Quickbooks

(A beginner guide for bookkeeping and accounting for small businesses.)

Table of Contents

Basic Bookkeeping for Your Small Business

Bookkeeping alludes fundamentally to the record-keeping parts of accounting. Accounting is the bookkeeping procedure (some would state the drudgery) of recording all the data concerning the exchanges and financial exercises of a business. What follows is an essential diagram of what bookkeeping for a small business involves:

Get ready source records for all transactions, activities, and different occasions of the company.

Source records are the beginning stage in the bookkeeping procedure.

Decide and enter in source records the financial impacts of the exchanges and different occasions of the business.

Exchanges have financial impacts that must record the business is in an ideal situation, more regrettable off, or possibly "unique off" as the consequence of its exchanges. The bookkeeping procedure starts by deciding the critical data about every transaction.

Make unique passages of financial impacts into diaries and records, with fitting references to source archives.

Utilizing the source document(s) for each exchange, the clerk makes the first, or unique, passage into a diary and then into the business' records. The diary passage records the entire transaction in one spot; at that point, each piece recorded in at least two records that are influenced by the trade.

Perform end-of-period methods.

These techniques are the fundamental strides for getting the bookkeeping records modern and prepared for the arrangement of the board bookkeeping reports, tax returns, and financial statements.

Aggregate the balanced preliminary parity.

This parity (a total posting all things considered) is the reason for planning reports, tax returns, and financial statements.

Close the books.

Bring the bookkeeping for the financial year finished to close and prepared things to start the bookkeeping procedure for the coming monetary year.

The Advantage and Disadvantage of Doing Your Bookkeeping

The issue of doing your bookkeeping got predominant with the appearance of ease bookkeeping programming in the mid-1990s. On September 27, 1994, Intuit accepted a program called MoneyCounts from Parsons Technology for $64 Million. Perceive changed the name of MoneyCounts to QuickBooks and made an exceptionally successful Unique Selling Proposition "You can set apart cash by doing your bookkeeping." That USP originated in Intuit, catching practically 85% of the small business advertising. Bookkeepers were no enthusiasts of this amazingly mainstream programming program for a few extremely legitimate reasons. Initially, it was anything but a good bookkeeping program with natural security defects. Second, it was proceeding unpracticed people take on an essential portion of the financial procedure. Third, it was diverting business proprietors from their center business, and last, it radically cut into the bookkeepers business.

Tending to the entirety of the issues concerning DIY bookkeeping in strange detail would need a book. I will cover a similar number of the principal items here to give the peruser a chance to increase a superior understanding of a critical subject. I respect any inquiries and remarks regarding the topic trying to help business people that might not have had the chance to settle on an educated choice appropriately.

The Issues

In case you're perusing this uncommon report, chances are you're one of the considerable numbers of small business proprietors battling with the issue of "doing your books." For some, holding an outdoor clerk or bookkeeper to handle your financial matters is comparable to opening up your wardrobe to a total stranger. I accept that this issue of an individual security is legitimate. Honestly, one reason I chose to turn into a CPA was that I realized I would be in business and needed to be in charge of my accounts. Most business visionaries don't have that choice or the range of abilities. The issue of DIY bookkeeping is of equivalent significance since it could influence the financial reasonability of the endeavor. There are various issues to address, including:

- The utilization of bookkeeping data to get ready tax returns
- The honesty of the economic data delivered
- The legitimacy of authentic information to spread future outcomes
- The administration of pay
- The expense of holding an expert
- The time, exertion and displeasures of keeping your books
- Tending to the administration's expanding inclination to audit
- The time and effort finding out about bookkeeping
- Making the bookkeeping methods
- The trust aspect

As should be obvious, there is many issues to address in relaxing on the precise decision. This is by a wide margin, not complete. There might be numerous other lawful, financial, and individual subjects in the inquiry. The point here is that the topic of creation and keeping up a lot of books and records for a small business is vital. The choice concerning how it will do ought not to be made spontaneously or by the ignorant. An individual working a small business doesn't have a sign of what they don't have a hint. Operating a business accompanies specific duties and pledges. Not knowing is not a legitimate explanation when the books and records fall into question. I present that as a business proprietor, you must know just what the issues are and become peaceful on an educated choice about nurture to each concerning them. You are, as a matter of sequence, the President of your organization, which accompanies the entirety of the related duties, including tax, legitimate, and individual liabilities.

Reasons and Excuses

Most, if not all new companies assume the errand of making their arrangement of books and records for a couple of primary rights:

- No assets to hold an expert
- The constrained measure of exchanges
- Uncovering individual financial data
- The observation that it's simple
- The penchant for hesitating
- Dread

The Facts

Each business must record a tax return. In the end, the issue of bookkeeping must tend too. A large number of people decide to set up their tax returns, which are another issue without anyone else's input. Let me address that before going further. It's a genuine, humble one and not because I get ready tax returns but since of the multifaceted nature of the tax laws, together with Federal and State.

I can look at the option of an individual setting up their tax come back to pulling out my teeth. At the point when I was a kid, my teeth turned out generally. I didn't need to drive to the dental professional to have them pulled expertly.

Irrespective of whether I dragged them out when I shouldn't have, inevitably, my permanent teeth would develop in to conceal my varied up conviction that I was a dental specialist. As a grown-up, I distinguish better. Ideally, on the off chance that you own a business, you know better. To endeavor to set up your tax return would be equivalent to attempting to be your dental specialist.

There is mostly a lot in question. Possibly missed benefits or far and away more terrible, over forceful discounts bringing about an audit and the sad slip-up of not joining your business and discovery your resources for a claim, to give some examples. If you haven't made sense of my situation regarding this matter, let me make it understood. Doing your tax return is a fantastic misstep. If you are going to start a business, you have to enroll in the appeal of a decent tax bookkeeper.

Returning to the do it without anyone's help bookkeeping issue, another reality to consider is the financial angle. This is legitimate as most new companies have zero assets in any case. Investing in proficient direction takes specific astuteness. One interesting point is the mainstream "Free discussion." I don't know numerous experts that would not offer an underlying system session to a potential new customer. That essentially makes this issue invalid and void.

If you choose to hold the expert to direct you, they will understand the financial issues included. The ideal individual will sustain you and your new business and concoct a valuing structure that will work. Try not to anticipate that a decent bookkeeper should work for nothing and don't enroll a relative or companion that is eager to work for nothing. They won't regard you like some other customer for the straightforward reality that you're most certainly not. A portion of the most noticeably awful customers I at any point needed to work with were loved ones. The issue is that on multiple occasions, I was the carrier of exceptionally terrible news, placing me in a precarious position. The off chance that you have a companion or relative that is in the business request that they allude you to one of their partners. You will all be cheerful, you did.

The rest of the issues all truly have to do with your outlook. Dread, delaying, discernment, and so forth all must tend to at the mentality level, and I'm not able to address those issues so I won't. Business and individual attitude mentors are in bounty today.

Twenty years back, when Intuit executed the misinformed USP that "You can set aside cash by doing your bookkeeping," business training was not standard. It was presumably more in the domain of psychotherapy or business counseling, which was either in the classification of very close to home or unreasonably costly for a startup. Today treatment and business training are standard admissions making the issue of outlook a point of - would you say you are not kidding about this business or not?

That remarkably leaves one residual issue to address, which is the volume of exchanges. Does it genuinely bode well to look for the assistance of an expert clerk when the amount of your transactions is insignificant? This inquiry prompts another inquiry, which is, what establishes negligible? On the off chance that it's not insignificant, would it be a good idea for you too, in any case, be doing your books?

Presently I can genuinely get into the topic of whether a business proprietor ought to do their bookkeeping. Permits first beginning with the meaning of accounting. It appears glaringly evident that a subject so significant to a business should characterize to settle on an educated choice on the issue appropriately.

The meaning of bookkeeping:

The work or ability to keep account books or deliberate records of cash exchanges (recognized from bookkeeping).

This is from your lexicon website

The meaning of bookkeeping is keeping a nitty-gritty record of the business exchanges for an individual or business.

A case of bookkeeping is the way toward recording bank statements every month.

So it's exceptionally straightforward. Or on the other hand, right? Where does one beginning? What technique for keeping records is worthy? What is the reason for bookkeeping? For these answers, I will allude you to IRS Publication 583 Starting a Business and Keeping Records.

Why Keep Records?

Everybody in business must keep records. Great records will assist you in doing the accompanying.

Screen the advancement of your business.

You need great records to screen the advancement of the business. Logs can show a demonstration of whether your business is improving, which things are selling, or what transforms you have to make. Great careers can enhance the probability of business achievement.

Set up your financial statements.

You need great records to get ready precise financial statements. These incorporate wage (advantage and lousy luck) statements and asset reports. These statements can help you in managing your bank or loan bosses and assist you in dealing with your business.

A salary explanation shows the payment and costs of the business for a given timeframe.

A financial record shows the benefits, liabilities, and your value in the business on a given date.

Distinguish wellspring of receipts.

You will get cash or property from numerous sources. Your records can distinguish the wellspring of your receipts. You need this data to isolate business from nonbusiness receipts and taxable from nontaxable salary.

Monitor deductible costs.

You may overlook costs when you set up your tax return, except if you record them when they happen.

Set up your tax returns.

You need great records to set up your tax returns. These records must help the salary, costs, and credits you report.

What Makes Bookkeeping a Good Career Choice?

Bookkeeping has become a profession in its title within the last ten years. It's increasing in demand in Australia, the UK, the USA, Canada, and New Zealand. This has been thanks to a variety of things, specifically the rise in small businesses and, therefore, the legislative compliance placed on small businesses.

Most of the countries anywhere bookkeeping has been cumulative in demand have a VAT, GST, or other federal, state, or local tax. Thanks to the increased compliance, small business often finds it's necessary to use someone to handle the day to day bookkeeping. This is often sometimes due to the business owner not having the knowledge or time to urge the experience required by government departments on time and accurately accounted for.

Bookkeeping has slowly increased its professional rankings thanks to the new compliance and necessity of business owners needing these specialist services. More and smaller business owners are turning to bookkeep staff to undertake their requirements, as traditional accounting staff is too expensive to rent on an endless base.

This has created a growing industry for bookkeepers to be involved. It's a specialized area, but not so dedicated that it requires a few years of coaching. Theoretical education is vital in credits, credits, and, therefore, the accounting equation to know how bookkeeping works, but it also requires the work experience to understand how auditing for various organizations works.

If you're curious about becoming a bookkeeper, it certainly may be a career choice, which can provide you with a future career. Additionally, if you're looking to start your own business within the future, it certainly may be a career choice, which may support those ambitions. You'll have flexibility and control over your hours and wages once you freelance as a bookkeeper. You'll create a little business from home to fit your personal needs, and it doesn't take tons of capital to determine. This makes it tremendously accessible for working parents as a home business special.

Sometimes persons fall under bookkeeping by helping a loved one or acquaintance do their books. Occasionally people start as a receptionist or accounts work and gradually combat further responsibilities. Other times people undertake a study to become a bookkeeper straight out of faculty. It's a career that may progress both form education or from experience. Either way, it's an exciting career choice. Legislation changes, roles change, and therefore, the more legislation, which is in situ to regulate small business records, the extra work a bookkeeper can provide discovery.

Is Outsourcing Business Bookkeeping a Good Idea?

Situation

Each new and existing business has the prerequisite to keep a trustworthy and complete arrangement of organization books and records. As the demands on the hour of business proprietors relentlessly increment, the choice of where to invest time, vitality, and cash becomes additionally testing. This is moreover confused by the way that most business proprietors don't have the fundamental abilities and understanding concerning business bookkeeping for them to capability play out this work to the standard required. By what method should this circumstance be handled?

Alternatives

As the business proprietor battles with the need to deal with their business bookkeeping, they have to think about the accessible options. The decisions are to either play out the accounting or to re-appropriate it to another organization. How about we survey these choices regarding their dangers and advantages.

Dangers

How about we direct our concentration toward the difficulties the business proprietor may look in taking on their bookkeeping work. To start with, consider how qualified are they are to have the option to manage business bookkeeping. If they come up short on the foundation to be effective at it, are they ready to take appropriate preparation? There additionally is a period factor - is there an ability to submit the measure of time required to figure out how to perform business bookkeeping appropriately and instantly? The expense as far as the money will be moderately negligible; anyway, there will be the need to go through cash to figure out how to do bookkeeping, notwithstanding the open door cost of time.

On the off chance that the business proprietor feels anxious concerning any of these variables or maybe they would prefer not to do the bookkeeping, at that point, considering different alternatives would be ideal. The next chance is to have an expert, either an individual or firm, handle the bookkeeping. Even though there can be an apparent and evident advantage of not being troubled with the business bookkeeping, there are inherent dangers. Dangers that should give a business proprietor delay to consider if redistributing is directly for them. The main hazard is giving secret business data to a person who is an outsider.

Regularly this kind of choice can boil down to how agreeable the business proprietor is with this individual and the level of trust in giving them access to business data. This is generally an informed decision. In other words - there is no assurance with anybody. Another hazard would be the cost in question. Is it moderate? The expenses of redistributing can be exceptionally high, particularly for quality work.

In conclusion, there is consistently the danger of trusting the individual handling their business bookkeeping is playing out the work in a correct, hopeful, and subjective way. These remarks to recommend there is nobody capable enough to perform business bookkeeping there are numerous who are uncommonly gifted for this work; it is only significant for the business proprietor to know about these dangers. Like any choice, there are additional advantages to every one of these alternatives.

Advantages

The advantages business proprietors get from re-appropriating bookkeeping are evident and worth considering. They remember the capacity to center their time for center business exercises that may incorporate advertising, obtainment, customer contact, HR, among numerous others. Breathing easy in light of the information that an expert is handling the business necessities and keeping the business proprietor advised of essential data concerning the organization accounts is critical. These are both all around upheld explanations behind employing an expert.

At that point, there are advantages of the business proprietor taking on their bookkeeping work. There is a desirable angle that all business proprietors should think about playing out their business bookkeeping. The ideal aspect is learning and understanding their business better from a financial point of view. Indeed, it is notable that business proprietors will get a shared understanding of their business when they can identify with their bookkeeping. Why? Being near the business, especially in managing cash, they can make canny conclusions from this data.

The ideal approach to accomplish this is to understand the bookkeeping procedure (that stretches out into bookkeeping perspectives) and how it identifies with business exchanges. Understanding this cycle and knowing where the numbers originate from is profoundly significant and significant. Likewise, knowing this data direct is far best than merely depending on what different clerks, bookkeepers, or experts clarify - regardless of how capable and proficient they are. Numerous new business proprietors settle on the decision to play out their bookkeeping. The explanation is regularly they think that its more financially savvy, particularly for the time being, and they value the advantages of personally finding out about the business from a numbers standpoint.

It is shrewd to look for proficient direction in setting up and learning the bookkeeping procedure. There are a few quality hotspots for bookkeeping guidance that ought to consider. Skilled instructional classes and subjective counsel and backing are perfect for learning the fundamental parts of setting up a legitimate business bookkeeping framework.

Importance Of Bookkeeping Outsourcing

What is bookkeeping re-appropriating? It is the procedure wherein you delegate your bookkeeping undertakings to a specialist group or person. Regardless of the idea of your business, bookkeeping re-appropriating can end up being very handy for you as you get master services at reasonable expenses. A large portion of these outsourced groups utilizes the most recent advances that you couldn't have managed something else. Bookkeeping redistributing ends up being helpful for you as far as cost, time, ability, and dependability. Here are the top advantages that you get from this:

Gifted aptitude

Bookkeeping is a significant strenuous exercise; it takes a lot of persistence and the specified range of abilities to finish this activity. If you don't do this appropriately, you can get into a great deal of difficulty from administrators. If you need to get a prepared master to do your bookkeeping assignments and need to spare expenses also, the best alternative is to depend on bookkeeping redistributing. You need to pay an ostensible charge to the re-appropriating and bookkeeping organization for the services rendered.

Convey time for profitable purposes

One of the significant advantages of bookkeeping re-appropriating is that you don't have the strain to deal with your records on schedule. Since you have appointed this obligation to an outside office, you have sufficient opportunity to focus on different parts of the business. Re-appropriating and bookkeeping give you enough time to concentrate on advancements and productive systems for your business.

Cost reserve funds

Bookkeeping redistributing is where you delegate the assignment of dealing with your book and records on low maintenance or per-venture premise to specialists who have a lot of involvement with this field. The costs that you pay as an expense to these outside bookkeeping re-appropriating organizations are very notable when contrasted with the pay rates that you have to pay to a full-time bookkeeper.

Unwavering quality

At the point when you select accounting re-appropriating bookkeeping to a specialist, you can have confidence that your records are in talented hands. These specialists are exceptionally dependable as they have productive involvement with this division. By falling back on bookkeeping re-appropriating, you get a high level of mental harmony, with which you can continue with your different assignments.

Speedy goals

During pressure circumstances, where you are in earnest need of getting your books arranged in time for audits and detailing, redistributing bookkeeping will push you, all things considered, as the outer master staff gives you snappy goals.

Small Business Bookkeeping Is A Moral Way To Maintain Records

Running a business isn't a child's play. Moreover, management small business bookkeeping is again a Herculean task. We all are alright conscious of the very fact that managing and maintaining financial records consume many time and personnel resources. Hence, there's one solution that will solve a drag of bookkeeping for little businesses. What's bookkeeping, and the way does it help in saving time and money? The answer to your query is that accounting may be a process that involves maintaining records of the separate transactions that have taken place throughout the year.

The functions of small business bookkeeping include rummaging through the entire revenue, profit, loss and expenses, dates of the transactions, and many other minute financial details incurred by the corporate. This brings us to the assumption that bookkeeping is one of the foremost vital aspects of a business regardless of its size. Small business bookkeeping must be maintained more accurately because once they know their financial status alright, they will consider expanding themselves. Small business bookkeeping provides many advantages of sustaining financial records. It assistances the owner or a manager in understanding the accurate financial status of the corporate business, and small business bookkeeping also helps these small businesses to know the exact financial position that further assists them in understanding the profit and loss that the company is arising. It furthermore helps these businesses to be financially and legally precise.

Small business bookkeeping contains the small print, like the daily transactions, business, loss if any, and other such details as these particulars can help small businesses to urge loans. Maintaining small business bookkeeping is additionally an enormous task like maintaining bookkeeping for any business. Therefore, it's always vital to recommend professionals who are thorough with their work, albeit the job is finished small business bookkeeping. So, hurry and call a little business bookkeeping executive to advise your task wiped out no time. Hiring professionals to try to accounting helps the companies to know their financial position because it further helps it to produce and also keeps a soundtrack of the bookkeeping of the business.

Small business bookkeeping should do daily because it helps to take care of the financial records regularly. The chief provided by the small business bookkeeping will maintain the daily transactions because it helps to stay track of the littlest of the monetary expenses or gains. If there's a hindrance within the regularity, then it'd become a serious issue leading to losing the path of the small business bookkeeping, causing loss to the corporate. It is often done either manually or with the assistance of computers. The essential purpose of the accountant or bookkeeping service is to take care of an accurate record for the corporate. This is often usually done by maintaining a monthly spreadsheet of the expenses incurred daily and another to point out the sales, purchase, gross, and net income. Small business bookkeeping is of great assistance to a business, and this has proved repeatedly, and it's indeed the most straightforward thanks to excluding unwanted troubles.

What is the Role of a Bookkeeper?

Numerous individuals confound the occupations of a bookkeeper and a bookkeeper, mainly since bookkeepers are now and then alluded to as accounting experts or accounting representatives. While fundamentally the same as, a bookkeeper centers around keeping up auspicious and precise records of financial information - extending from pay, installments, deals, and buys. A bookkeeper, then again, takes the data recorded by the bookkeeper to make financial statements. Since the occupations entwin, a few bookkeepers start their professions as bookkeepers.

Bookkeepers frequently utilize one of two strategies for recording financial information. The twofold passage technique, while complicated, guarantees a lot of books that liberate from botches. It uses an adjusting arrangement of credits and charges isolated by two particular records inside the books. The single passage framework is significantly less confounded and is frequently the strategy for decision for small businesses. Information is kept up in an income and cost diary and uses accounts exclusively of pay and cost.

There are a few unique books that use for recording financial exchanges. The daybook uses to record the subtleties of a transaction, however not all businesses look after daybooks. A few organizations decide to use diaries. The information from the logs is then recorded in records as indicated by their relating class of buys, deals, money, credit, and so on.

All records contain various zones so they would then be able to be utilized to make the financial reports, including the economic history and the pay explanation. Documents can use for recording any classification. Businesses usually have client records (or deals records) where they track exchanges with clients. They likewise have providers records (or buy papers) where they can follow their transactions with their providers. The overall record will remember information for the organization's benefits and liabilities, pay, and costs.

A preliminary parity organizer utilized to enable a bookkeeper to check the books for any errors. The chance that the charges and credits of every record don't coordinate, the bookkeeper knows there is a mistake. When utilizing the twofold section strategy, the praises of exchange must offset with the charges. The bookkeeper isolates the charges and credits into two sections up until a specific date, building a worksheet that subtleties every record's parity.

Bookkeeping is certifiably not an essential occupation, and the errand isn't one that does rapidly. Most organizations require at any rate one full-time bookkeeper, and considerable organizations must have a few bookkeepers. In any case, smaller businesses may redistribute bookkeeping work by hiring support to handle this activity for them. At the point when a bookkeeping administration use, a bookkeeper will put in a couple of hours seven days at the organization, taking a shot at the records and being satisfied that the books remain in balance.

What Exactly Does a Bookkeeper Bring to the Table?

If you run a business, you've likely got a DIY mentality. This suggests you think it's possible to try everything yourself; otherwise, you don't trust people to finish a selected task. Therefore, you'll tempt to get accounting software, like QuickBooks, and take responsibility for your company's record-keeping. However, savvy entrepreneurs know what a bookkeeper can do for them and haven't any hesitation hiring an expert. As such, we explore the positive impact of bookkeepers below.

Spotting Errors

Businesses that hire bookkeepers soon realize they're not as well-off as they thought. There are countless samples of organizations that operated without a bookkeeper for years before finally taking the plunge. What usually occurs in these belongings is that the bookkeeper cleans up records that wrongly mingle assets and expenses, reviews purchases for duplications, and pays bills on time. Also, as saving corporation money by spotting mistakes within the books, a bookkeeper can save little business thousands of dollars a year by ensuring late fees never got to be paid.

Allowing for attention on Business

When you try to stay your books so as, you're spending time faraway from your business, usher in a bookkeeper, and permit him to handle day-to-day tasks, like ensuring new employees file the right paperwork for payroll, submitting invoices, and paying bills. Your bookkeeper also will track company expenses and ensure all costs are correctly entered into the software to make sure the business is preparing for tax time.

What does this mean for you? Also, as knowing how your expenditures fare against your budget, you furthermore may release time to consider what you are doing best, which is running the business. Your bookkeeper spends a couple of hours every week tidying up, which suggests you've got extra hours to make new products, marketing existing services, and usually helping your business grow.

Ensuring Trust during a Partnership

If you're during a business arrangement sort of a partnership, a bookkeeper is essential. Albeit you think you've got an excellent relationship with a business partner, things can quickly turn sour if there are any misconduct accusations made with regards to bookkeeping. All it takes is one accidental error from either party to make a rift within the relationship that becomes irreparable.

When you hire a bookkeeper, both parties are often satisfied that there's no conflict of interest. A bookkeeper is an independent third party that will perform all the required company transactions quickly and efficiently so your business partnership can remain as strong as ever.

Put, a bookkeeper will guarantee accuracy and permit your business to interact in pre-tax planning. The quantity you would like to pay in taxes is going to be accurate, and early payment means no possibility lately fees. In particular else, a bookkeeper enables you to specialize in running your business safe within the knowledge your record-keeping is being taken care of by an expert. If you're unsure about your internal bookkeeping process, it's going to be time to talk with knowledgeable.

Bookkeeping Services or Accountant Services - Which Do You Need?

The term accounting covers an entire spectrum of services. Wikipedia defines accounting because of the production of monetary records about a corporation. The principles of accountancy apply to account, finance, bookkeeping, and auditing. Accounting first created in Mesopotamia, where people used accounting methods to record the expansion of crops and herds. Over thousands of years, it's grown into the complex systems that we see today to match the requirements of companies, governments, and financial institutions.

So let's check out what types of bookkeeping and accounting different. Both are concerned with the financial accounting of a corporation. However, that's anywhere the similarity trimmings.

Using the symbol of a tree, Bookkeepers are the roots of the tree. They supply the inspiration for making an honest audit trail of the day to day financial operations of the corporate. These activities would include:

- Recording of the day-to-day financial transactions of a corporation
- Fixing a sound economic file system supported the set standards of either double or single-entry secretarial.
- Integration cash accounts and booming all ledgers to the balance stage
- Providing the business owner income and price information to assist them support and grow their business

- Reviewing data and categorization for preparation handy done to the accountant
- Assisting in constructing a compact financial team for his or her business, i.e., accountant, payroll preparation companies, etc.

Accountants are the trees. They take the knowledge that the bookkeepers provide and make reports and analysis to assist the business to get financing, put a worth on their business, plan for the longer term, and steel oneself against tax reporting. The word "accountant" derives from the French word "computer," which suggests to count or score. Accountants often assist business owners in creation decisions about what sort of company they need to make - sole proprietor, corporation, indebtedness corporation, partnership, etc.

The limbs of the tree are the various quite accounting services available to help with business and private financial planning. A number of these would include tax preparation, cost accountants, business valuation, and forensic accounting.

For a little business owner, the utilization of a bookkeeper daily is a crucial step. This may give them a sound foundation (rather than keeping the receipts during a box) and save them money at the end of the day. Many business owners today prefer to do their bookkeeping, employing a spreadsheet system or software. This is often an excellent plan as long because the right training provides so that they understand the fundamentals of accounting and, therefore, the functioning of the software.

Outsourcing Small Business Bookkeeping Efficiently to Manage Finances

Small businesses have started outsourcing their bookkeeping needs because it takes part in at least one of the foremost every day and yet multitasked responsibilities to handle records of usual transactions and obtain to understand how a corporation owes or what proportion is owed to them by these other organizations. Additionally, bookkeeping stays as a crucial part of managing financial flows within the corporate though it also keeps business owners too busy handy over these sorts of the task while stepping into the projects at an equivalent time. As a result, more business owners are transferring this task to virtual assistant companies who are specializing bookkeeping through the years, plus saving lots of on in-house costs.

What is bookkeeping in general?

Bookkeeping encompasses an entire lot of tasks included in financial record keeping: from records of kit, inventory, accounts payable and assets, income statements, balance sheets, financial statements to income statements and other bank transactions. Additionally, it takes to specialize in keeping track of those essential documents, so all finances are seen and in situ. Without those to manage and organize bookkeeping tasks, some information is going to be easily lost, and thus, every single account that doesn't tally will cause inappropriate expenses and losses, which can turn profits unnoticeable enough while the business grows.

Indeed with outsourcing, bookkeeping is going to be tons more comfortable to manage as more and more companies are helping entrepreneurs in several parts of their businesses. Albeit it gets into the risky process of profits and losses management, entrepreneurs won't anymore need to spend time worrying about recording information because these outsourcing providers are going to be ready to enact your accounting systems to end things as soon and credible as possible. Now, if you are going to outsource bookkeeping tasks of your company today, here are three necessary steps to possess a fresh and straightforward start without fear about your expenses:

Step 1: Always Be Consistent

Consistency is the initiative for you to make sure that your accounting has been working a similar way for each month. As you will be transferring this task to your service provider, confirm that even a change in the set of columns manages to stop adjustment of computations, which will pour in several results. Inform your service provider also intimately every detail on how your program works before getting them handy over it. Otherwise, you'll learn the opposite way around by having them introduce their accounting to you while you, on the opposite hand, should be ready to apply your accounting to them through certain agreements and confirm all information stays equal and tallying on each side. Once an organization is maintained, having mismatched information is going to be impossible to require place.

Step 2: Keep All Good Records

Many businesses will often miss out on tax benefits yearly because some information is missing, plus having nothing to function a backup for the deserved deductions. To unravel this issue, systems provided by your chosen service provider will quickly be showing you the leads to a clear and accurate manner without finding other information from an outside source. Like your accounting applied within the program, allowing them to also keep relevant documents or papers by scanning receipts and organizing them in one place too. Labeling on folders is a method to raised distinguish which is which and which should check out first as they need specific titles.

Step 3: Maintain Invoice Strategy

Setting invoice integrity is going to be as simple as this: together with your bookkeeping service around, they will quickly have an eye fixed on open invoices that are needed to account and closed appropriately because it should not be floating there for long. Otherwise, without proper management on getting invoices filled at the appropriate time, this may bring the cashback to the corporate and be starting again to handle expenses and fund future projects.

One way to affect this is often setting an invoice policy. Having your bookkeeping provider to affect different transactions held within the business, you will get them to manage your invoice policy to encourage people to pay on time and stop getting an excessive amount of charge. For instance, they ought to supervise invoices that ought to pay within 15 days. Alternatively, customers are going to be ready to face the penalty behind it.

Small Business Bookkeeping Is Challenging

Keeping your bookkeeping needs organized by outsourcing is one of the foremost challenging areas in managing your small business because it would always mention how LIQUID your business is while you're continuing to create on more projects to continue receiving profits and letting it grow. Indeed, you would not want to double your effort or maybe waste any of your investments - be it on time or money, but you'll get to enjoy every free time you experience through the assistance of your bookkeeping service.

On the opposite hand, as you stay because the lead director of all things, having them on your behalf shouldn't leave you only accepting stuff because it is, but you will have to check on accomplishments regularly. Build up their responsibilities by requiring them to submit regular reports and allowing scheduling meetings wherein you'll talk on sudden changes or maybe minimal problems to fix as soon as possible. This way, you'll not only make sure the health of your business financially but your good relationship together with your service provider, so you're both giving within the best for the company - everything's kept worthwhile!

Things to Look for in a Bookkeeper

After you've got resolved to outsource your accounting for your home business, you would like to pick a bookkeeper. In the selection of a bookkeeper, there are several essential elements to believe. It's necessary to travel with a bookkeeping service that will offer the simplest level of assistance along with side value for your money. Beyond this, however, you'll find several other points to believe when finding bookkeepers.

One of many essential elements to seem at while checking out a bookkeeper is the exact market-linked experience. Undoubtedly, the longer the bookkeeping service you're seeing has been in business, the higher. Additionally, it is also crucial that you find a bookkeeping business that comes with dedicated experience in working for similar organizations or fields. When you are a small business, hire a firm that's familiar with handling small companies instead of one that works with corporate associations.

You should also search for a bookkeeper that's adaptable concerning offering services which may design to match your company's specific preferences. As an example, some bookkeeping providers accompany packages which could not work with what you need during a bookkeeping service. Do not forget to form inquiries to make sure you'll be entirely satisfied.

One of the compensations of employing a bookkeeping service is the opportunity to enhance your processes and save time. For that reason, you ought to be able to relax a touch over paperwork, fines, and output deadlines. To accomplish this, you would like to settle on a bookkeeper that's competent in successfully managing such things in your part.

About this, you want to search for a proactive bookkeeper that's entirely trustworthy concerning being at the highest of all kinds of things and can ensure they line up of all essential documents from you by expected output deadlines.

How simple can they be to contact? Along the way about the technique of checking into likely bookkeeping providers, make sure to ask them how and also when it's easy to speak with them. Get a bookkeeper who is adaptive and ready to ask you during the Saturdays and Sundays and within the evenings. This is often getting to make lifestyle much simpler for you.

Last but not least, confirm you select a bookkeeper that would assist you in saving tons on the value of offering their advice to you and taking care of your books. Bookkeepers that have the most uncomplicated capabilities and practice need to assist you in saving tons of additional money at the end of the day.

We like to figure we can gain proficiency with any expertise it takings to run an organization that may be legal for some business proprietors, yet for others figuring out how to do the books appropriately can be a gigantic test. Hiring an accountant might be useful for the bookkeeping-tested. Here are ten desires a business ought to need to ensure an accountant will have the right stuff to be a piece of the group.

1. An accountant must have an understanding of the 10,000-foot view. At the point when you buy a bit of gear, a clerk must know the idea of setting up the benefit and risk records and the ability to dispense the installment to intrigue cost and obligation head decrease.

2. Have an essential understanding of the five fundamental kinds of documents. The accountant ought to have the

necessary knowledge of the distinction between resources, liabilities, value, salary, and costs.

3. Deal with all the easily overlooked details that have to do with financial activities. The clerk must be meticulous and ready to concentrate on the easily overlooked aspects which empower the big things to deal with themselves.

4. Great relational abilities. The clerk must be happy to request an explanation or help on the off chance that they don't understand something. Correspondence is necessary to your understanding of what's occurring with the bookkeeping without being the one doing the everyday work.

5. They should have a considerate of the three fundamental financial statements. Benefit and misfortune, asset report, and income statements ought to be made available to you through the tenth of the next month by the accountant.

6. A clerk must be PC proficient. This indeed abandons saying. Gone are the times of responsibility books by hand. An accountant should be comfortable with bookkeeping programming and be knowledgeable about Word, Excel, email, and the web.

7. An accountant must be happy to proceed with their instruction. Your clerk ought to focus on upgrading their abilities with classes or self-study. It is significant for them to keep awake to date with the bookkeeping aptitudes any business requires.

8. An accountant needs to have a fundamental understanding of your industry. Every industry has various terms and insider perspectives that must learn at work. Ensure an accountant has a general knowledge of your industry.

9. Understand how to do appropriate employment costing for the business. Things and occupation detail must follow all

activity costs. This is basic to realize how a lot of an undertaking genuinely costs. It is critical to have the option to rely upon the clerk's data is exact and reliable.

10. An accountant must be eager to do a substantial duty to your business. Discover somebody who is happy to focus on your business and is centered around completing things in a promising way.

Set desires for an accountant before you employ them to guarantee the business will work beneficially. To know where your business is successful, you should have the option to depend on the books and the accountant. Guarantee the success of your business by hiring an accountant as a feature of your group. Great financial records are a piece of the way to success, and a decent accountant can help clear that street.

Outsourcing Bookkeeping
Activities and Tasks

Every year businesses are needed by law to publish their financial documents or reports. During that point, financial experts and bookkeeping professionals play an essential role as they create that report more accurately and precisely. Accounting is one particular section of a business that takes care of a number of the foremost tedious tasks. Hiring the bookkeeping services of some good bookkeeping companies or bookkeepers gives you the sensation of being more efficient since business people see that an inevitable part of the expansion of the business and that the enjoy of having annual financial reports and support the superb decision. Stand back from all types of monetary risks which will harm your business and obtain your accounts books and financial bookkeeping tasks managed by some expert bookkeeping or accounting persons or other tax firms.

The situation has changed nowadays. Big and little companies alike outsource accounting, financial services, and similar functions routinely to low-cost destinations like India. Bookkeeping may be a domain that has been witnessing tremendous growth, particularly during the past few years. It's and offers immense possibilities as small business entrepreneurs with strong sales abilities often need some full-time bookkeepers to research the accounts books. However, such bookkeeping services have little to try to to with the number of product sales. They need far more to work with the various levels of accounting activities like invoicing, bill payment, payroll processing, and, therefore, the like. Companies that have already got full-time bookkeepers are likely to save lots of about $40,000 a year by taking to bookkeeping services offered by highly competent accounts service providers in these countries.

Bookkeepers also provide a direction for the business owners who would be making crucial decisions supported the business' bookkeeping details and company's accurate financial standing. It's thanks to this reason that the correct maintenance of bookkeeping tasks has become significantly important. Since business entrepreneurs require their employees to specialize in other primary business operations, many entrepreneurs prefer hiring other third parties that provide excellent bookkeeping services and leave behind the task of maintaining proper bookkeeping records to those accounts professionals.

Bookkeeping persons are expected to understand everything they need to understand. This is often difficult even for them at first, but at the end of the day, you can't figure with them at that level. They have to know the importance of this area of accounts by bringing this subject up frequently in their first consultation itself. The bookkeeping assistance is maximized without dalliance or atrophy extra money on getting these bookkeeping errors fixed. While they're watching the clerks, the CPA would be watching them both. The occurrence of fraud may be a less likely phenomenon during this arrangement. The CPA does what they are doing with a minimum level of adjustment. Within the end, the business owner gets timely and accurate financials monthly, which is the most vital intention and aim. Anyway, within the maintenance of bookkeeping accounts, accuracy is required. Accountants, also as bookkeepers, take this into due consideration.

Here's Why Small Businesses Should Tap Bookkeeping Services

Business people know the estimation of accurate bookkeeping; however, with such a significant quantity on their plates, it is problematic to be a one-person group who maintains the business, deal with minor subtleties, or maybe following the cash going in or out. Proprietors of small businesses who need a bookkeeping administration can either procure an in-house clerk or redistribute the work to a bookkeeping administration organization.

How we work together has changed with the accessibility of innovation. Bookkeeping administrations help businesses with their backend needs, for example, appropriately checking creditor liabilities, money due, uses, benefits, or misfortunes, among other pivotal bookkeeping worries of your business. A bookkeeping administration can do this without being genuinely present in your office. Here are some top advantages of redistributing your bookkeeping needs:

No Headaches, More Time

Doing all the bookkeeping without anyone else or in-house will be the time that isn't spent admirably. The time you will dedicate for such undertakings can be spent considering showcasing your business, creating new items, improving procedures, among others. At the point when you enlist a bookkeeping administration, you can invest more energy contemplating how you can improve your brand, accomplish your objectives, or disturb the business and impact essential changes.

Financially savvy

If you will procure an in-house illustrative to do all the bookkeeping undertakings for you, at that point, be prepared to pay more. Remember to remember for the condition advantages to fund, finance taxes, retirement plans, debilitated leaves, medicinal protection, among others that you are required to do by law for your representative.

At the point when you enlist bookkeeping administrations, you can obtain them on a for each errand premise or pay them hourly, week by week, or month to month contingent upon your requirements and concurrence with them. Everything will rely upon your needs, the size of your organization, and the measure of work that should finish.

Specialists Doing What They Know Best

Accountants will do bookkeeping best. Not excessively, you are terrible in numbers but rather let us state that it is ideal to leave these things to the specialists. Bookkeeping administrations have groups and groups of bookkeepers and accountants that realize what they ought to do in any event, when they are half snoozing. The exceptionally gifted clerks will be there to handle every one of your questions and concerns. What's best is that they won't score their heads; however, give answers and arrangements that can assist you with maintaining your business better.

Clerk versus A Team of Bookkeepers

At the point when you restructure your bookkeeping needs, you are essentially tapping a decent pool of abilities that can help each other to serve your brand. What's incredible about this is it won't cost you as much when you procure a comparable number of bookkeepers or accountants to work in your office.

Adaptability is additionally a non-issue when you redistribute your bookkeeping requirements. As your business advances and as your needs differentiate, a bookkeeping organization can without much of a stretch change following them as they as of now have the labor and frameworks to do as such.

Quality Work

Numbers are everything for bookkeeping administrations. They live by the numbers, and quality forms are set up to ensure mistakes are maintained a tactical distance from no matter what. Recollect that bookkeeping blunders can cause significant cerebral pains for business proprietors and you need to maintain a strategic distance from that by framing a decent association with a bookkeeping administration with the best individuals to carry out the responsibility and the best advances and frameworks to ensure everything is as precise as could reasonably be expected.

Knowing the Difference Between a Bookkeeper and a CPA

Most small business proprietors begin with a good thought and an enthusiasm for what they plan to offer general society. They may spend incalculable hours sorting out themselves to at long last open their ways to the general community. For most of the individuals, the initial not many months can be frightening, a rite of passage, maybe. As time passes, the proprietors find out increasingly more about what works and what doesn't work as far as pulling in potential customers and bringing deals to a close.

Ideally, the organization got their work done before opening their entryways and found that their business will have tax commitments that they never had as people. If the organization is a company, at that point, they should pay themselves as W-2 workers. This implies the organization will retain finance tax from the representative (basically themselves) and need to pay the organization's half too. At that point, there are reasons that the organization can make to bring down their tax obligation. Now and then, findings can make yet are neglected by occupied business proprietors. Things can get convoluted rapidly, and before you know it, that smart Quickbooks program the proprietor purchased can transform into quicksand, sucking the most valuable item any business proprietor has, time, directly out.

At some point or another, most organizations go to a bookkeeper to deal with their financial record keeping. A quick web look for a bookkeeper utilizing Google will return thousands of CPAs, Independent Accountants, and Bookkeepers. Now, you may be confounded and ask yourself, what's the distinction? For what reason do you think

I composed this article? A clerk commonly does the chronicle of all every day financial exchanges and their appropriate order. A few accountants will likewise offer different types of assistance, as the arrangement of financial statements, finance handling, quarterly tax filings, and annual tax planning alongside different administrations. A clerk that gives those administrations is going about as an autonomous bookkeeper, that is, a bookkeeper that isn't contracted by the State like a CPA is.

In contrast to a clerk or an autonomous bookkeeper, the CPA (Certified Public Accountant) can play out an audit just like any of the different assignments that the others can perform. Sadly, for general society, in numerous states, only one of those three experts who can publicize themselves as a "Bookkeeper" is a CPA. Makes you wonder precisely how robust their anteroom is, isn't that right?

Turn into a CPA, an individual needs to take a specific number of ace's level courses in bookkeeping alongside their college classes which didn't need to be business-related. At that point, that individual can either sit for the state CPA test quickly and then work under the supervision of a previously authorized CPA for a long time, or the other way around. It is, without a doubt, a long and monotonous procedure, and they will charge you appropriately (understudy advances don't come modest). That is all okay, and without a doubt, any individual who gets themselves through that sort of scholarly investigation is deserving of regard. No one is contending against that. Be that as it may, as a purchaser, I'm expressly searching at the best cost and the individual who will take care of business right. Indeed, CPAs are exceptionally instructive, however, would I truly like to follow through on high costs to somebody who went to class for ten years only for my bookkeeping? My answer is resonating no. (Particularly when a few accountants are profoundly qualified. Some even hold Master in Business Administration (MBA) degrees).

There are obviously, organizations out there that require the blessing that accompanies an authorized CPA's audit of their financial statements. An organization that is hoping to get speculators locally available to contribute a great many dollars, for instance, will need a CPA to approve their financial statements to facilitate any speculator trepidation. Somebody who is hoping to get an amazingly enormous credit from a bank (99% of small businesses doesn't approach banks for advances worth a large number of dollars) is additionally going to require a CPA to direct an audit. Most small to medium measured business proprietors will never require a review led by a CPA. Regardless of whether they needed an inspection from a CPA, that doesn't mean they can't make one utilize the financial information accumulated by a clerk or a free bookkeeper.

A CPA is just going to check and approve the work previously done by the clerk (and charge thousands of dollars for his mark). Most CPA's don't do the genuine everyday work that clerks do. They either have accountants they keep on staff to do that work, or they redistribute the bookkeeping work to a bookkeeping organization. So for what reason would anybody need to address ludicrously significant expenses to a CPA to complete their bookkeeping for their small or medium estimated business?.

In all decency, I can perceive how somebody with no information on the bookkeeping business would feel more secure going with the CPA. He has the degree, the large office, and the eminence to dazzle any small business proprietor's socks off. In all actuality, however, any self-regarding, dedicated, genuine accountant can do similarly as great of an occupation if worse than that extravagantly estimated CPA at a lot more attractive cost. Actually, on the off chance that you've at any point had your bookkeeping done by a CPA, at that point, chances are the work you saw was finished by a reliable accountant. My recommendation to anybody searching for a bookkeeper is to spare yourself a great deal of cash and give your financial record-holding obligations to an expert accountant who offers different types of assistance I referenced already too. The odds are that you won't just show signs of improvement cost, yet you will get better client support since organizations like yours are a clerk's meat and potatoes, not only a supplemental wellspring of pay as most CPAs see their bookkeeping customers be. That, however, you will probably build up a durable association with your clerk and have an incredible resource in your group. I trust you have made the most of my post for the afternoon and stay tuned for additional to come.

Questions You May Have About
Outsourced Bookkeeping Services

Bookkeeping is an errand that an organization needs to perform regularly. Accounting implies that you are recording and following the entirety of the exchanges in any event, when they change for the day — any exercises record in the proper diary account. The making of diary passages just as other money-related statements are one of the first things which a lot of business proprietors can't understand, so it is then essential to get comfortable with the chance of outsourced bookkeeping services. If you need assistance with bookkeeping, outsourced bookkeeping services can be the response for you.

Should Your Business Look Into Outsourced Bookkeeping Services?

It isn't uncommon for a business proprietor to be somewhat skeptical before enquiring about outsourced bookkeeping services. The choice of redistributing can be one of the most troublesome ones that a business proprietor will ever make when investigating the development of your business. Be that as it may, indeed, as a business proprietor, you have to designate some work to be successful. That you attempt to do everything yourself, you will, before long, find that you genuinely have no opportunity to do whatever else. Outsourced bookkeeping services might be the response for you.

What Information Do You Need From Bookkeeping Services?

The choice of the privilege outsourced bookkeeping services will rely upon the information that you get from them. You ought to pose inquiries as bookkeeping is a significant piece of your business. Most importantly, you ought to get some information about the safety efforts which the organization takes to keep the information private, particularly while on the web. You need to ensure that the protection guidelines that the organization follows are the equivalent followed by businesses in the United States. You ought to likewise be getting some information about quality as you need the best work done.

How Are The Services Rendered?

There are two kinds of organizations that you have to know with regards to outsourced bookkeeping services. The first would be a seaward bookkeeping firm and the other one, a nearshore bookkeeping firm. A few organizations will offer assistance in nearshore territories, which implies one district, for instance, North America. A seaward firm can be found anyplace else on the planet. You have command over which organization you need to utilize. Going with a seaward organization will, for the most part, give you similar quality and a much lower cost.

Would you be able to Eliminate A Backlog?

Small business proprietors more than likely won't have any desire to spend the cash on a significant information passage group. That is because it tends to be over the top expensive. Outsourced bookkeeping services, then again, can be significantly increasingly reasonable. These organizations effectively possess the most significant information passage groups, and a portion of the organizations will likewise have branches wherever on the planet. The groups in the various departments can interface using the web, so all the backlog that you have should be possible very quickly. That is significantly more helpful than some other alternative you may have.

What Does It Take to Become
a Bookkeeper

A bookkeeper is an accounting proficient who keeps up a few or the entirety of an association's financial information. For the most part, the duties of a bookkeeper change dependent on how small or huge the association is. Most bookkeepers keep up a business' overall record, henceforth the activity title. A general history monitors charges and credits, by and significant income, resources, risk, costs, just as increases and misfortunes. In a small association, a bookkeeper may handle all accounting capacities, including creditor liabilities and receivable. In a significant association, they may have unmistakable duties identified with the overall record or other accounting capacities.

Regardless of what number of duties a bookkeeper handles, practically all businesses require those intrigued by this occupation to understand the full extent of bookkeeping. The prerequisites to turn into a bookkeeper incorporate some preparation or training. Numerous bookkeepers can prepare at work. However, the developing pattern towards an association's financial records being increasingly straightforward has prompted managers looking for candidates within any event a partner's degree in control, for example, accounting or money. Winning a degree to be a bookkeeper can likewise build business openings.

Preparing or instruction, for the most part, envelops general training, the executives, and accounting coursework. The general practice incorporates English creation, school-level mathematics, and variable based math. The executive's courses comprise business morals, financial aspects, advertising, and authoritative assembly. Accounting and commercial courses include many types of accounting, finance, taxes, and information frameworks. Higher degree programs spread different parts of accounting and fund, including revealing, research, insights, and propelled contemplates in accounting techniques and standards.

To be a bookkeeper additionally requires some close to home properties and enthusiasm for the field. Bookkeepers must have the fitness for math because the activity requires doing figurings much of the time. Solid PC aptitudes are additionally significant because practically all associations keep up their financial records and reports utilizing accounting programming. A few managers require broad information using explicit accounting programming bundles and different kinds of utilizations that consolidate a lot of a business' necessary information utilizing those applications. Since the activity requires exactness, substantial regard for subtleties is another characteristic needed for those keen on this occupation.

Bookkeepers can likewise win accreditations, for example, confirmation from perceived associations. The American Institute of Professional Bookkeepers then the National Bookkeepers Association both offer tests for bookkeepers. These kinds of associations create morals and comprehensive strategies for bookkeeping. Breezing through the test brings about procuring confirmation, which can likewise expand work openings.

A bookkeeper pay can fluctuate significantly depending on the sort of boss and obligations of the activity. Experienced bookkeepers, for the most part, procure higher wages. A few managers additionally reward those with a degree, by expanding their pay. As a rule, the standard fee for bookkeepers was roughly $36,000 every year, as indicated by the Bureau of Labor Statistics.

Why Go For Bookkeeping Firms?

Bookkeeping manages to abridge the information identified with the current financial situation of your business. Dealing with your records and sorting out your financial information is essential to assess how well your business is progressing. For some businesspersons, especially the novices, bookkeeping appears to be tedious and chaotic. Some contract experts in commerce with the activity; however, that can be costly. Others go to bookkeeping firms, which is a lot smarter alternative. There are countless bookkeeping firms in the United States. Bookkeeping services offered online also. Be that as it may, on the web and disconnected have their upsides and downsides.

Online versus Offline Bookkeeping Services

- Your bookkeeper can, short of much of a stretch, visit your business locales in a disconnected framework. An online bookkeeper can't impart just as a disjointed contracted proficient or somebody from a firm can.
- The disservice of a disconnected bookkeeper is that you have constrained options. The strategy is to arrange poorly, and you need to pick somebody who works inside nearness. In this manner, internet bookkeeping services might be a superior choice concerning where your business is and what decisions you have.
- In the web-based bookkeeping services, there is an enormous danger of misrepresentation and trickiness included. There may be a cheat, and you will be unable to follow the specialist organizations after that.

- For disconnected bookkeeping, hiring an expert can be costly. You need to experience a problem of experiencing applications and surveying the candidates and making determinations. The entire procedure is tedious and keeps you involved. In this way, while you are utilizing, you are not selling your item or building compatibility with the clients.

You may need to give extra advantages to the worker. More regrettable, the worker may leave for superior activity, and you need to begin from the significant scratch. What could be more unpleasant?

Working with bookkeeping firms tackles the issue of hiring an expert and the danger of trickiness that includes. With bookkeeping firms, you can have your financial information abridged and introduced rationally and transparently without stressing over the unwavering quality as the organizations assume contend liability of the tasks. These organizations employ specific staff, and painstakingly chose experts. Great bookkeeping and bookkeeping firms have elevated expectations of training and confirmations that should meet. You can quit stressing as the information is in safe hands, and you can have your financial reports deliberately created and introduced to you. Good Luck!

Why You Should Use
QuickBooks Bookkeeper

The QuickBooks Bookkeeper application is probably the best thing that can happen to your business the off chance that you are hoping to streamline your bookkeeping exercises to upgrade its benefit. Manual bookkeeping is troublesome, and any minor mix-ups can prompt the fate of your business; however, numerous organizations think that it's troublesome changing from manual to auto bookkeeping.

Notwithstanding, the framework accompanies a gigantic expectation to learn and adapt that can appear to be scared to the average individual who has no involvement in it. Fortunately, there are a few different ways to successfully execute this bookkeeping application to support your business regardless of whether you have no clue about it. One alternative is to redistribute the utilization of the user to another firm, which is knowledgeable with the use of the application for the bookkeeping procedure. You can likewise, on the other hand, utilize the services of a specialist to prepare your staff to have the option to use the QuickBooks Bookkeeper effectively.

The points of interest that can get from the utilization of the QuickBooks Bookkeeper programming are colossal. Right off the bat, the use of this product guarantees that you won't spend significant available time on bookkeeping exercises and instead utilize an opportunity to put resources into progressively beneficial business adventures like structure and improving client connections.

The utilization of this product additionally implies that you can utilize fewer workers, who might some way or another have accused of regulating your organization's bookkeeping exercises. Decreased quantities of workers will mean lower operational expenses and a smaller compensation bill. Different advantages incorporate speedy and straightforward access to financial information, standard business books, and financial reports just as standard business forms and secure access to hierarchical information.

The QuickBooks Bookkeeper likewise accompanies highlights that can be modified to suit the necessities of your business, so regardless of what sort of business you are associated with, this application will be helpful for you. It prescribes that you get this product to deal with your bookkeeping exercises in the beginning periods of your business to forestall any difficulties later when the volume of tasks gets gigantic.

Bookkeeping Education Opportunities

The financial record of any business or organization is critical for tax and money related purposes. Attempting to precisely record all information to have formal documentation on cash exchanges makes up the field of bookkeeping. Through instructive examination, understudies figure out how to add to a business by working with their assets.

Solicitations, bank statements, payslips, and finance uses are a few zones recorded by a bookkeeper. They record this information in a general record, which permits them to deliver a financial explanation for directors accurately. Working through a degree program leaves understudies with few instruction choices.

The college degree choices include:

Certificate Program

This is a typical method to get familiar with the necessary information to turn into a bookkeeper. Since experts right now expected to have a comprehensive information base, an authentication program will cover accounting procedures as well as the utilization of the business' PC programs. A math-based educational plan coordinated with business techniques and financial aspects is likewise centered around. Coursework on business law, finance, and mechanized accounting are a few themes talked about over the length of an authentication program. Numerous understudies decide to get ensured through the American Institute of Professional Bookkeepers to increase a serious edge to have more enormous business openings.

Associate's Degree

Numerous understudies choose to work through a partner's degree program to pick up the best readiness to turn into a bookkeeper. With the number of comparable activity obligations and information expected to perform accounting, understudies can enter a degree right now well. Entering a bookkeeping degree or accounting degree typically comes down to what undergrads are joining in. A bookkeeping degree centers around a similar material; however, it may separate it into increasingly brought together courses. The courses finished incorporating general training, fundamental PC instruction, and seminars on taxation and PC accounting. Understudies will find that whether they select to try out an accounting or bookkeeping partner's degree program that they will get similar training and have the option to enter a vocation as a bookkeeper.

Run of the mill courses in a degree program include:

Bookkeeping

The course shows understudies twofold passage accounting that users inside a business. The practices to settle accounts with a bank explanation secured alongside finance issues.

Taxation

Finance taxes are securing as to accounting strategies. The prerequisites for recording all government, state, and neighborhood fees and net salaries are accentuating.

Managerial Accounting

Understudies will apply their insight into accounting information and use it to make an essential plan for a business' accounting framework.

Encouraging instruction can be gotten yet frequently is just sought after by understudies that need to change into turning into a bookkeeper. Understudies can work through a program in two-years or less and step into a business and become a bookkeeper. Exploit tutoring and begin preparing to record every single financial store for a company. Licensed bookkeeping schools offer various ways relying upon the profession's objective of understudies. Full accreditation is the grant to programs that provide quality training by offices like the Accrediting Council for Independent Colleges and Schools.

Switch to Online Bookkeeping Services

You are a small business proprietor, and you realize that bookkeeping is a fundamental piece of the business. Yet, you likewise recognize that it is tedious and enhances the client. As it were, it is a crucial insidiousness. It turns into a much higher persistent issue for you if you are utilizing an obsolete offsite accounting administration who is messaging or faxing you refreshes once per week, or more terrible yet, you bought costly bookkeeping programming for your office to find that it doesn't have the adaptability that you requirement for essential reports.

And the chance that that is the circumstance that you're in, you ought to truly consider changing to a web-based bookkeeping administration and begin receiving these rewards immediately:

1. Classification and control

Numerous business proprietors who are not utilizing a web-based bookkeeping administration refer to their dread that the entirety of their financial information is gliding around on the internet and can effortlessly hack by any individual who cares to attempt. That is much the same as saying you won't put cash in a bank since it may ransack. The present security innovation and secure servers make the web probably the most reliable strategy to trade information. Your records remain classified, and the primary individuals to approach will be those that you award a secret key to, and still, at the end of the day, you can confine what an individual can see. For instance, the chance that you have an individual doing charging and assortments for you, you can constrain their entrance to only those capacities, and that's it.

2. Openness

Since your bookkeeping records are on the web, you can get to them from any place that has an association if you have to keep an eye on something before you go out to go to the workplace you can. On the off chance that you are with a customer and need to survey a receipt, giving there's an association, you can bring it up immediately. You are not secured in a single PC to get to your information, and clearly, you don't need to hang tight for a week after week update from the accounting administration.

3. Coordination

The chance that your bank on the web, most web-based bookkeeping services, can download your financial records straightforwardly into your bookkeeping framework — discussion about help. The entire thought of an online context is to use the information it stores to streamline redundant assignments and lessen the number of copy passages that must make. Bookkeeping occupies enough time for what it's worth, web-based accounting can make a generous imprint in that time.

4. Customization

Your business and your administration style are one of a kind. Wouldn't it be a smart thought to have the option to collect your financial information in an arrangement that fits the business as opposed to providing the company with a standard configuration? Web-based bookkeeping permits you to do only that.

5. Debacle recuperation

Periodically small companies don't give this potential wrecking issue any; however, substantially less have a plan to manage it. On the off chance that you have accounting programming on your PC at work, you may be running day by day reinforcements, however; then you need to store those plates somewhere offsite. That is a reasonable practice provided that your office endures a debacle, or your PC mainly crashes; at that point, in any event, you have the information to begin once more. With online services and their gigantic server ability and constant reinforcement, you never need to stress over a calamity destroying your records.

6. Improved client support

Since your online framework is recording and computing progressively, you can offer continuous responses to clients with questions. If your financial information incorporates into the structure, you have the most recent information on installments got, and discounts gave.

7. Advertising machine

With the discretionary projects accessible, it's conceivable to make your bookkeeping framework and income winning instrument. As of late, a few structures have coordinated email showcasing programming that exploits your client and merchant records as of now in the framework, and that can convey proficient email promoting pieces and track their presentation. Search for more advancements that enhance information as of now in your structure.

Advantages of an Online Bookkeeping Service

Customary bookkeeping is a dreary assignment that most business proprietors don't have the tolerance or mastery to do. While trying to set aside cash, some even attempt to keep up their books themselves, yet since they don't have the wise for the activity, they wind up depending on off base financial statements, regularly demonstrating sad to their business at last. Right now will show you the insight behind re-appropriating your bookkeeping needs to an online specialist co-op.

1. Recover the heap off your

Believe it or not, recover the collection of yours. That you can move the weight of record-keeping to a web-based bookkeeping administration, you can trust, why not? Along these lines, you can essence on what you excel at, and that is maintaining your business.

2. Concentrate on bringing in cash

Since the heap is away from you, you can focus your time and vitality on producing income. You are not a bookkeeper or a bookkeeper, so why sit around idly on an action that won't make you any benefit?

3. Let an expert carry out the responsibility

Except if you have a solid accounting foundation, the odds are high you will wreck your books. Letting an expert carry out the burden for you will guarantee that your financial information introduces precisely. Try not to change your business by going about as the inside and out smarty-pants who makes attempts to do everything yourself

4. Cost adequacy

With an internet bookkeeping administration, you pay for just the hours you have to keep up your books. Anyway, with an in-house bookkeeper, you should pay somebody 8 hours every day, five days per week, in any event, during reasonable periods. A web-based bookkeeping administration permits you to pay for services just when you need them.

5. Access to excellent Accounting programming

Web-based bookkeeping services approach the most recent versions of top-rack accounting programming, which would demonstrate costly if you need to buy it yourself — also the expectation to learn and adapt to figuring out how to utilize it.

6. day in and day out online access to your books

Web-based bookkeeping services will guarantee that you have an off-website reinforcement of your books accessible 24 hours per day, seven days per week. You generally approach your financial information, even in a hurry.

7. Information security

This is significant because your books are the existence of the blood of your business. Chance that there is something that you can be distrustful about, this is it. The present internet bookkeeping services are outfitted with 128-piece information encryption to guarantee your financial information shelter on the web.

8. Responsibility

You can generally pursue the online specialist organization on the off chance that they mess up with the activity. Or on the other hand, you can usually retain installments. If you do it without anyone else's help and chaos up, you have no one to fault yet yourself.

9. Unlimited authority

You can generally end the agreement and pay just for the measure of work once it's finished — no compelling reason to procure a full-time bookkeeper and stress over compensation and legitimate advantages.

10. Access to the best specialist organizations

Since a ton of business proprietors are finding the upsides of redistributing their bookkeeping needs, there is an assortment of online services to browse. You should pick the best.

Advantages of Outsourcing Bookkeeping For All Businesses

Redistributing bookkeeping services is these days the propensity in numerous businesses. That is the reason there are likewise increasingly reallocating organizations right now turning out to be exhibit in the market. These organizations enlist experienced bookkeepers to concentrate on specific services like bookkeeping and accounting so they can give them to the organizations that want to redistribute. Re-appropriate methods subcontract, so it implies away from the organization's perceived office. For customary businesses, bookkeepers as often as possible experience a firm preparing. After a timeframe, they are then attempting to apply what they have realized and do the standard bookkeeping services, generally in recording and staying with the's books of record.

Re-appropriating bookkeeping is a superb measure for organizations to keep up accurate records in their books. This is for the explanation that accounting requires proficient abilities and a much-engaged endeavor that can be conveyed uniquely by a specialist who is knowledgeable about the field. A precise bookkeeping administration improves the ability of a firm to concentrate on business development while at the same time abridging dangers and expenses.

If you incline toward Outsourcing bookkeeping, so you get more points of interest like:

- Cost sparing
- Offloading assignments
- Getting aptitude
- Getting greater innovativeness into the activity

- Increasing critical thinking
- Looking for most noteworthy consumer loyalty
- Keeping the business working every minute of every day

If you pick redistributing bookkeeping, you decline the labor you have, and yet you get similar services offered by these customary bookkeepers, also that you likewise find a good pace different costs identified with having these bookkeepers around, including the preparation costs. It is like a contract somebody has the accounting division of your business.

If you need to maintain your center business easily so proper bookkeeping is essential prerequisites. Along these lines, redistributing bookkeeping gives you immaculate bookkeeping answers for any business.

Choose Your Quickbooks
Bookkeeping Company With Caution

There are numerous reasons why business visionaries favor redistributing QuickBooks bookkeeping. This administration especially pulls in small business proprietors who either need time or bookkeeping aptitudes. These small associations additionally endure deficiency of staff as a result of significant expenses of keeping up a US-based bookkeeper. The normal rate for a US bookkeeper is generally $45. This rate contains the additional cost of keeping up with them in your office. For example, your full-time bookkeeper merits ergonomic office furniture and gear.

They are additionally qualified for paid leaves, free preparing, and regular execution evaluations to give a premise to their advancements or compensation raises. Redistributing QuickBooks bookkeeping will permit you to get to many exceptionally skilled bookkeepers. What is considering all the more astounding about these free assistants is that they work remotely. They will never trouble you in the workplace. These organizations have completely prepared workplaces, and they cause their overheads alone. This is the reason they guarantee to have the capacity to decrease 50% of your office consumptions.

Their rates are entirely reasonable, dangerous, and alluring to small business proprietors. While redistributing QuickBooks bookkeeping, you ought to be cautious, however. There are web-based QuickBooks experts who wind up charging you more than your in-house bookkeeper does. They cause you to bring about the expense of setting up programming. This can extend somewhere in the range of 395 and 495 dollars. They additionally sell you a record on their server, which could cost somewhere in the field of 70 and 100 dollars. On the off chance that you add the above-evaluated expenses to their hourly rate, which is somewhere in the range of 35 and 45 dollars, you will perceive how uncalled for these organizations can be.

As expressed above, you should be exceptionally cautious when picking redistributing QuickBooks bookkeeping firms here in the US. The most reasonable activity would utilize USA accounting firms that have auxiliaries in Asia. This mainland has numerous exceptionally qualified experts who know about the US bookkeeper's morals and standards. They have prepared to keep books like American experts. The main distinction is that these seaward QuickBooks specialists are progressively practical. That you need to free your opportunity to concentrate on overseeing different zones of your business, at that point, re-appropriating QuickBooks bookkeeping intends for you.

It is additionally the ideal answer for those of you who have over-burden or awkward bookkeepers. Redistributing QuickBooks bookkeeping guarantees you complete fulfillment regarding velocity, results, and client care. Since the keeping of the book is a non-center capacity, you can easily redistribute it. The outworking isn't keen on your clients. Their advantage is in your small business. They need to assist it with developing by handling the bookkeeper's job, which is general protract, delicate and tiring.

Since your quality requires in India, for example, time that you would somehow use for supervision is naturally opened. Since you additionally don't need to venture out to the distant goal where your administrative task is handling, you can consequently set aside cash for other pending undertakings. Everything that your specialist co-op is doing at some random time can see online progressively. Innovation can permit this. In the wake of redistributing QuickBook bookkeeping, you can catch up on the advancement on Skype, online life, email, or moment talk massagers.

Benefits of Outsource Bookkeeping and Accounting Services

Bookkeeping is one of the most essentials of any organization. It is liable for overseeing and following financial tasks and help to settle on economic choices. Bookkeeping services are slanted to name an assignment that is to track exchanges that experience each day. Any business, regardless of whether enormous scale or medium-scale constrained level, things like the bookkeeping records are difficult to store legitimately.

Accounting is a significant assignment for small and enormous financial firms. Bookkeeping and accounting give financial solutions and strategies that can be helpful for every single business. In any case, bookkeeping must do cautiously. Bookkeeping and accounting is the reference over which one can think about the demand for the organization.

Many accounting firms offer particular bookkeeping services permitting you to invest your valuable energy concentrating on your business. Regular bookkeeping services help small businesses to set aside time and cash with legitimate record keeping. Many accounting specialist co-ops presently use QuickBooks programming, to oversee money due and creditor liabilities, invoicing, bank compromises; documenting quarterly taxes, check compromises readiness, and assortments.

Bookkeeping services are of two sorts. First is the manual bookkeeping, and the other is registered bookkeeping. On the off chance that one is maintaining a small business, at that point, the person in question can deal with the company through manual clerking. Notwithstanding, if you have a standard moderate size or a large market, having picks automated bookkeeping will be perfect for you to keep your business.

These days accounting should be possible on the web, and along these lines, anybody can utilize the web-based bookkeeping offices. You should consider how web-based bookkeeping services can be better or advantageous from customary bookkeeping services? Continue perusing to know the advantages of web-based bookkeeping and accounting:

- Less Expenditure
- Quick Work
- Fewer Requirements
- Contract a devoted Accountant
- Correspondence Facility

If you need to spare time for the principle procedures of your business at that point, re-appropriate your accounting services is the best choice. In the wake of re-appropriating these bookkeeping services, you can likewise concentrate on other significant procedures of your business. In this way, presently, you need to pick the best bookkeeping specialist co-op who can serve you the exact bookkeeping services.

What is the Difference Between Bookkeeping and Accounting?

What is the contrast between bookkeeping, accounting, and accountancy? When somebody says they are an accountant, would they say they are a bookkeeper? Does it genuinely make a difference?

Bookkeeping

Bookkeeping is the procedure of methodically recording the financial exchanges of a business, to show how the exchanges identify with one another. Accounting is, to a great extent, a mechanical procedure and doesn't include any investigation of the financial transactions, yet instead the account of them.

Generally, the records were kept in a book, henceforth the name bookkeeping. Nowadays, accounting is ordinarily performed utilizing a bookkeeping programming bundle. However, the names of the books (daybook, cashbook, diary, and record) are as yet used.

A bookkeeper's capacity is fundamentally one of recording exchanges in the diary and presenting on the record and is now and again alluded to as a records assistant.

There are two sorts of bookkeeping: single passage and twofold section. In single section bookkeeping, the record of every exchange conveyed to either the charge or credit segment of a solitary career. In dual section bookkeeping, two passages of every transaction are sent to the record: one to the charge side, and one to the credit side, of the relating account. This is so the two sections can use to check one another.

Accounting

Accounting is the deliberate chronicle, revealing, and examination of financial exchanges of a business. As bookkeeping contains making a financial record of business exchanges, it is consistent with the state that the job of bookkeeping is enveloped inside the extent of accounting, and the bookkeeping framework utilized by a business would shape some portion of the accounting framework.

Accounting likewise incorporates the planning of statements concerning resources, liabilities, and the practical consequences of business.

Accountancy is the occupation identified with accounting, and an accountant is an individual who does, or if nothing else is answerable for, the work. Accountants regularly represent considerable authority in a specific region of accounting, for example, taxes, auditing, or executives.

In a small organization, the entirety of the bookkeeping and accounting assignments likely could be performed by a solitary individual. Right now, individuals would ordinarily be alluded to as an accountant.

How to Choose Among Bookkeeping and Accounting Services

Bookkeeping and accounting, all in all, view as a similar arrangement of services. In business terms, bookkeeping is the view as a subset of accounting services. An individual assigned the situation of an accountant ought to be acquainted with bookkeeping services. In any case, a bookkeeper need not realize all the undertakings performed by an accountant.

A business dependent on its size must pick between two sorts of services to follow a proficient methodology towards the fund related issues. The accompanying conversation separates between the two arrangements of services to assist you with picking the best experts for every one of them:

Characterizing the Two Processes

Bookkeeping is described as the arrangement of services that keeps up the accurate records of business exchanges with the goal that the upper-level administration can watch out for the inflow and surge of cash.

Accounting, which otherwise called financial accounting, is the arrangement of services utilized to complete an intricate examination of the general financial circumstance of an association that includes bookkeeping as a small piece of it.

An Elaborate View of Duties

You can additionally find out about the contrasts between the two by understanding the assignments performed by a bookkeeper and a financial accountant. A bookkeeper's obligations are increasingly centered around the everyday financial circumstances of an association. This includes:

- Reconciliation of bank exchanges of the organization to keep away from or perceive any extortion is happening in the organization's financial balance.
- You are managing representative finance while remembering the administration guidelines of the area.
- They are keeping records of records payable, just as records receivable.
- You are keeping track of the stock, which is influenced by the buys made and pay created by an organization.
- Above all, the readiness of the overall record and financial statements. A bookkeeper must guarantee that all the business accounts are precise and forward-thinking.
- An accountant doesn't play out his obligations on an everyday premise; instead, he surveys the overall record and financial statements arranged by the bookkeeper toward the finish of a month or a quarter and, additionally, toward the finish of a financial year. The accompanying extensively arranged obligations are a piece of an accountant's activity profile:
- An accountant examines the financial records and reports arranged by the bookkeeper to enable the top administration to settle on new choices for the development and benefit of the business.
- A tax arrangement is a significant capacity of an accountant. Estimation of taxable pay and derivations are the significant undertakings for which an organization depends on an accountant.

- Budgeting is another significant movement for which a business house needs the services of an accountant.
- An accountant likewise fills in as a counsel to the organization during occasions like mergers, acquisitions, and all other new business choices.

It is a great idea to think about an accountant as a manager to a bookkeeper. The last should answer to the previous, so the general procedure of business accounting is followed successfully.

As should be obvious, the obligations performed by a bookkeeper are more repetitive than those achieved by an accountant. Then again, an accountant has a refined arrangement of services to play out that help the business to have a control on its benefits and generally to speak financial soundness.

Which Services Are Required?

Presently the inquiry is how a business ought to pick among bookkeeping and accounting services. As referenced above, it is the size of the company that should shape the premise of the kinds of services required by it.

Small businesses don't produce a massive volume of solicitations and bills, and in this manner, can function admirably with both of the two kinds of services. An accountant is undoubtedly the more reasonable option for a small business, as he can perform the two types of assignments. Hiring a bookkeeper for a small business may not be of extraordinary assistance in methodology like tax arrangement and significant choice taking.

Undoubtedly, there is a requirement for the two kinds of services. It gets significant in a large organization to diminish the weight of an accountant with the goal that he can concentrate more on the considerable undertakings like business prompting and financial proclamation investigation. In this way, a bookkeeper must enlist to deal with day by day methods like record the board and representative finance the executives.

In numerous states, away from between the obligations of a bookkeeper and an accountant are made to help businesses of various sizes, pick the correct arrangement of services. These states unequivocally prescribe hiring the services of an ensured open accountant to account.

Advantages Of Off Shoring Bookkeeping And Accounting

With fast walks in media transmission, seaward business process redistributing is ending up being an essential device to numerous organizations. Hiring an organization that situates in another nation may appear to be minimal odd. However, it offers various focal points which the organizations rush to use. What began as redistributing of low end IT employments right off the bat in 1990 has now associated with itself whole business forms like accounting and bookkeeping. And the incentive of accounting redistributing today incorporates numerous advantages and not only reserve funds in labor costs.

These can be induced as under:

1) Access to rare ability: Talent pool in nations like the US are maturing and contracting. As indicated by a Bureau of Labor measurements, around 75 million gen X-ers are approaching retirement, while only30 million Gen X's can supplant them. The circumstance is the same for some European nations. In a situation like this, numerous organizations are battling to discover the accounting ability at a sensible rate. Offshoring bookkeeping forms take care of the issue for them.

2) Transfer of expenses and hazard to specialist organizations: Companies spend a great deal in hiring, preparing, and holding the staff. At that point, there is additionally the need for infrastructural offices to be dealt with. Organizations are gladly moving the expense and related dangers to seaward specialist co-ops who, for evident reasons, invest vigorously on staff advancement and

administration programs. Organizations are likewise, in this manner, saved the crucial administration cost in the running an in the house accounting division.

3) Multiple services under single stage: Another extraordinary bit of leeway that gathers to small estimated businesses specifically is that a business proprietor has the decision of utilizing the various services offered by these outsourced vendors. Since these organizations spend significant time in small business accounting, they likewise provide tax return services, finance the executives, ledger compromise, financial reports, QuickBooks reports, and so forth at a moderate cost. Any independent CPA would charge extensively for every one of these services.

4)Better use of financial assets: Through redistributing assignments, for example, accounting and finance, companies can diminish economic hazards by using financial assets shrewdly. For instance, an organization need not spend on an in-house accountant when all that is required is the administration of a bookkeeper. The redistributing of accounting services gives the organizations this adaptability of choice and better use of financial assets.

5)Reduced Overheads and incredible reserve funds: Companies can spare as much as $50000 per annum by supplanting an in house accountant with an outsourced one. Likewise, fixed overheads like finance costs and representative advantages can stay away from.

There are different advantages related to redistributing of bookkeeping services. A Company appreciates expanded investment funds as well as development in productivity and center towards its center business. So it is continuously a success win circumstance for an organization depending on the redistributing of bookkeeping.

The Role of Tax and
Accounting Services

The contemporary business situation is getting a charge out of the points of interest and dynamism gave by the re-appropriating industry-whether or not the contracting procedure is connected to tax and accounting services, HR, business accounting, or other center elements of the association.

Tax and accounting are some of the most significant elements of any business firm. Regardless of their tendency, size, or size of tasks, organizations employ accountants, payroll managers, tax consultants, and auditors to streamline the financial and administrative records of their everyday exchanges, bookkeeping forms, and other in house accounting needs and prerequisites. With the expansion in outstanding burden and number of business exchanges, these organizations are thinking that it's progressively helpful to redistribute this center capacity to proficient tax and accounting services suppliers.

Aside from making determined and experienced changes following suit customer demands, they likewise give access to best in the class foundation and programming backing to oversee private accounting information adroitly and in a quick way.

The re-appropriating market is flush with accounting and tax re-appropriating firms, which brag of experienced groups of qualified accountants - prepared in handling organization accounts and administrative compliances of differing extents.

The better part of these specialist co-ops is situated over the globe and gives proficient, brief, and top-notch services to meet the critical accounting and taxation necessities of everything being equal. They are well prepared to handle huge just the as small quantum of work and have an unemotional online nearness complete with redesigned accounting programming, cloud innovation, and best in class server emotionally supportive networks. They give a comprehensive rundown of services extending from the most necessary occupations like tax and return recording to the nonexclusive ones like payroll the executives, obligation bank compromise, planning of conclusive records and salary consumption statements, accounting of receivables and payables and other everyday information section work.

Presumed tax and accounting services suppliers are knowledgeable about handling specific errands, for example, VAT Service, Budgeting, Credit Card Reconciliation, Cash Flow Management, Inventory Reconciliation, Ledger Maintenance, and ensured taxation services.

The expanding levels of rivalry in the overall business and financial atmosphere have made it essential for business organizations to receive the most recent patterns of re-appropriating to improve their central concern figures and remain ahead in the race. Gifted sellers connected with rumored BPOs and KPOs have the capability of giving the best outcomes inside tight calendars and cutoff times and lead to substantial cost decreases. They assist organizations with adapting up to the expanded remaining task at hand during the weight time frames - leaving the assets and the executives allowed to address the more key capacities and issues on hand.

As the pattern of redistributing essential capacities past household limits is picking up confidence, an ever-increasing number of organizations are looking towards minimization of operational and value-based expenses, profiting altered tax arrangements and different services-the dependable and confided in the way.

Why Do Small Startup Companies Need the Expertise of Tax and Accounting Services Providers?

Are you considering beginning another business? Away from setting up the foundation and different business-related variables, the most significant territory of concern is commerce with the financial procedures and capacities. If you are very nearly beginning a small business with restricted capital, at that point, you are looking towards covering the assets to the most extreme by cost-cutting and tight planning. The situation being what it is, if you are an individual with a foundation in accountancy and an understanding of taxation runs, then you can without much of a stretch deal with this center zone alone. Be that as it may if you do not have the experience and aptitude in these regions, at that point, hiring a virtual controller or a firm for giving tax and accounting services is the ideal approach to save money on included expenses of hiring a full-time accountant.

The significance of the services of a virtual controller or outsider experts for tax and accounting services proves to be handy for the accompanying reasons during the beginning up the procedure when various moves are being made to make the establishment of a successful business:

1. The assurance of the business structure (Sole ownership, organization, LLC, or a Corporation) should be possible by getting an understanding of the upsides and downsides of each through the master assessment of an expert master, rather than utilizing inadequate information for the development of the equivalent.

2. The feeling and financial investigation of the virtual controller relating to the business plan goes far in giving a strong base to the startup.

3. The quantum of the exchanges decides the accounting programming that should be used by the tax and accounting services suppliers and virtual controllers. The appeal and help gave on the equivalent, and the conventions required in the opening of a financial balance for business purposes by the specialists help the first run through proprietors set things up the correct way.

4. The hiring of tax and accounting services causes the association to remain refreshed with the most recent updates in guidelines and rules identified with the recording of tax returns and relevant reports. Auspicious accommodation of mandatory financial statements and reports maintains a strategic distance from punishments and lawful issues.

Aside from the conventional bookkeeping forms, handling of related reports, arrangement, and accommodation of the last records, tax documenting, and so forth, the organizations giving tax and accounting services and the virtual controllers help in the development and union of the business over some time. Different manners by which they help the small business proprietors talk about underneath:

1. Supervising the payroll and installment services

2. Giving counsel on the tax advantages and installments that ought to make to the specialists over the year.

3. Assisting in the monetary parts of advertising and acquirement methodologies.

4. A virtual controller is generally a decent tax specialist, and his assessments help in sparing the costs that could have caused in hiring the services of a certified proficient.

It is significant for small businesses to fire up firms to reduce expenses at every possible opportunity, and redistributing the critical capacity of accounting and taxation into experienced hands helps the issue and additionally ensures precision and auspicious accommodation of consistent reports and financial statements.

Types of Business Management and Accounting Degrees

In case you're busy picking a suitable business program for yourself, you may realize that you have vast amounts of alternatives to look over. There are various degrees accessible at business schools, and among them is a business the board and accounting degree.

A partner's degree in business the executives and accounting is an incredible venturing stone to a business profession for people who are not ready to manage the cost of a lone ranger's program. Here's some useful information about the partner's degree in business the executives and accounting.

Course Duration

A partner's degree can be earned in around two years. A few schools may offer quickened variants of this program, permitting understudies to complete their coursework in under typical consummation time. Notwithstanding, such projects might be progressively escalated and give fewer breaks, so ensure that you are up for the test before you join.

As a result of its shorter-term, alumni of a partner's degree can join the workforce that much sooner. Investing less energy in school likewise implies understudies can save money on costs like settlement, transportation, stopping, books and supplies, and individual fees.

Also, business the executive's schools may much offer adaptable calendars for a partner's degree program. Some may hold classes at night, while others may permit understudies to take courses online to give them the alternative of picking the timetable and method of discovering that is generally advantageous for them.

Coursework

Coursework engaged with a business the executives and accounting degree are intended to give graduates a differing set of abilities and expansive base of business knowledge.

Such a program ordinarily consolidates courses in business ideas, board standards, innovation, and human sciences. In this way, you may end up learning points like accounting and business works on advertising, money, and enterprise alongside courses, for example, PC essentials and correspondence. The coursework additionally relies upon the focus you pick.

Contingent upon the school, you might have the option to pick intriguing fixations with your degree. For instance, a specific business, the executive's school in San Diego, offers accentuations like occasion planning and retail deals.

A partner's degree in business the executives and accounting, notwithstanding setting you up for passage level business positions, gives a perfect pathway into a lone wolf's business program. It might make you qualified for the finishing of a single man's projects that some business the executive's schools offer.

Profession Opportunities

A partner in business the executives and accounting degree can open the entryway to section level authoritative assistance supervisor positions. Graduates may likewise have the option to verify office supervisor positions in smaller businesses.

The center employment of an authoritative assistance supervisor is to assume responsibility for an association's tasks and ensure the association's capacities easily. Be that as it may, the particular obligations and duties of managerial help managers rely upon the degree of power they have and the size of the association. Alumni of this program may likewise have the option to seek after section level accounting or bookkeeping positions.

Accessible vocation openings rely upon the specialization you pick with your degree too. For instance, a local deals accentuation program plans graduates for the section to mid-level situations in local conditions.

When you've chosen to put your future right now, begin searching for business schools that meet your area and spending necessities. Get a rundown of schools in San Diego or whatever another city that you can see yourself living in for a couple of years and start the enlistment procedure!

Taxation and Accountancy Specialists

The specialty of accountancy or accounting, as indicated by the official definition, alludes to the estimation, articulation, or arrangement of financial information that is utilized by loan specialists, managers, speculators, tax specialists and other leaders in settling on choices in regards to the assignment of assets between and inside organizations, organizations, and open offices. Accounting is additionally characterized by some as the craft of "grouping, recording and abridging in a huge technique and as far as cash, the exchanges, and occasions which are financial in nature, character, just as deciphering the outcomes thereof."

Taxation is a financial duty forced on people and businesses, basically to back the tasks of government, just as raise assets for unique projects or undertakings. Tax may likewise use for other significant purposes besides simply raising assets. It could apply to debilitate specific exercises, for example, smoking or liquor utilization and perhaps a vehicle for moving riches starting with one gathering then onto the next, such as taxing the extremely rich to spend for welfare programs for poor people.

In nations like the United Kingdom, taxation may include installments to various degrees of government, for example, the local government, which is known as Her Majesty's Revenue and Customs and the nearby government. Personal taxes, National Insurance premiums, esteem included tax, partnership taxes, and fuel obligations are among the primary wellsprings of pay for the focal government. The worth added tax, or VAT, which is right now demanding at the standard pace of 17.5% on provisions of merchandise and enterprises, is additionally a significant wellspring of focal government income. This is a tax required on purchaser consumption. Another significant wellspring of government income is the company tax, which is requested on the benefits and chargeable increases of medium and enormous organizations. For company taxes, the basal rate is 30% and commonly required on taxable earnings above £1.5m. Nearby governments, just as the focal government, likewise win incomes from the personal tax, as each working individual has a specific annual fee imposed on them, contingent upon their month to month pay.

As per taxation specialists, the position to force taxes originates from two sources. The primary location arises from enactment passed by parliament, which is known as the 'resolution law.' These resolutions are likewise commonly distributed and give subtleties of any progressions or acclimations to current tax laws. These progressions are fundamentally proposed by the Chancellor of the Exchequer, as a rule in the spending limit, and then went into law by Parliament. Second, another significant authority is called 'case law,' and this is made from the choices taken in legal disputes. At whatever point taxation turns out to be very drunk and differences once in a while originate from the HM Revenue and Customs and taxpayers, these, in the long run, bring about legal disputes. The ultimate result came to these circumstances at that point turns into the "case law," which view as a significant impact in future rule law translations.

There is a lot of private consultancy firms that represent considerable authority in giving taxation and accountancy-related services to sole owner businesses, firms, or organizations. By and large, a taxation and accountancy consultancy administration may have clients going from people who claim a pastry shop or small store, to restricted organizations and significant partnerships, and they offer types of assistance that are custom-fitted to suit each organization or individual prerequisites. The variety of taxation and consultancy-related work may run from giving individual self-appraisal returns, enterprise tax self-evaluation, property pay taxation, Capital Gains Tax planning, Inheritance Tax, Retirement, and succession planning, Value Added Tax (VAT) planning and consultancy, Stamp Duty and different services. Another accountancy-related assistance may likewise incorporate giving records in a statutory configuration, accounting, payroll organization, giving spending plan and income figures, getting ready month to month or quarterly administration accounts, just as providing consultancy to beginning a business and giving talks on issues, for example, current illegal tax avoidance or hostile to misrepresentation enactment.

Where Do You Get Bookkeepers for Accounting Firms at Reasonable Rates?

You should be asking why accountants would require bookkeepers. They are undeniably expected to do it without anyone else's help. Well, indeed, however, not so much. It works a similar route as specialists and medical caretakers. Specialists are relied upon to know it all that medical attendants do, and yet their consideration is required on cases that attendants are not prepared to handle. For instance, a specialist is ready to regulate an immunization, and so is a medical caretaker. Be that as it may, the attendant isn't prepared to 'recommend' an antibody.

So also, an accountant knows to keep up books and can oversee it without a bookkeeper, yet a bookkeeper isn't prepared in accountancy. At the point when accountants get new undertakings, they relegate bookkeepers for the bookkeeping while they center around accountancy assignments like the arrangement of accurate records and undeniable financial reports. This is the typical pattern with CPA's and accounting firms the same.

In any case, frequently, it happens that proficient bookkeepers are very few. This makes them challenging to get, yet additionally makes their rates excessively expensive. Day's end, accountants turn down new businesses for not having bookkeepers. Dismal right?

You are thinking about whether there is an exit plan?

Fortunately, there is. It is conceivable through re-appropriating. Business Process Outsourcing today give bookkeepers to accounting firms at financially savvy rates. You should be thinking about how individuals to part with delicate information, for example, accounts, yet you would be amazed at the strategies followed by BPO's to solace such concerns.

Here are a couple of things they do.

Embrace a "No working for contenders" strategy.

Sign a "Non-exposure" concurrence with employees

Permit just limited web access to employees

Have an arrangement where employees are not permitted to utilize cell phones or information move gadgets, for example, pen drives, hard circles, CD's/DVD's.

Have severe passage/leave arrangement through Bio-metric unique mark get too.

Exceptionally secure methods of information move.

Such measures have extraordinarily limited the dread of re-appropriating, and many more individuals have discovered alleviation in it. Accounting bookkeeping services are additionally looking for following a ton nowadays.

Redistributing bookkeeping could be perhaps the best choice for CPAs and accounting firms since they stand to profit. Bookkeepers at accounting firms at costs so low are too acceptable an arrangement to miss. With this administration set up, accountants can take on the same number of new customers as they get. They never again need to stress overworking as a specialist without a medical attendant's help.

Bookkeeping For Accounts and Taxation Purposes

For each small-time business proprietor, the bookkeeping part is, without a doubt, an overwhelming weight. In any case, it is significant that he builds up a proficient bookkeeping framework from the beginning itself while directing business. Dealing with a business which consents to the laws and business prerequisites warrants the arrangement and upkeep of some composed agreement of accounting. For an accounting strategy to succeed, it is principal that some method of financial accounting like the receivables and goings set up, and that every one of these records presents a genuine bookkeeping picture for examination just as for tax purposes.

Bookkeeping is a crucial piece of a business; one can express various reasons like audit purposes, the arrangement of bookkeeping records, as a reason for vital dynamic purposes and planning of speculator outline and different archives. All said and done, and there are still a ton of small scale business proprietors that don't keep proper tabs on their business' financial part. This can prompt more significant cerebral pains when the tax staff comes thumping, in the end.

With the goal for somebody to keep up adequate bookkeeping records, one ought to embrace an arrangement of keeping the receipts just as check stubs as confirmations of salary coming in and going out. These archives must be aggregated day by day, entered into a significant spreadsheet, and must be petitioned for later references in like manner. This will undoubtedly empower one to set up a basic income account. It will show the monies coming in and the funds going out on an everyday premise. Keeping a tight tab on this can be of extraordinary help with managing the managerial piece of maintaining a business.

One needs to make a month to month benefit and misfortune account and needs to think about the income statements one has readied and some other financial information bits applicable to the business. Work out the gross benefit; in any case, by subtracting direct expenses of offers of merchandise from the all-out marketing projections. From that point forward, one may keep on finding the net benefit figure by removing every single other cost identified with the business, including warming and lighting, pay, and intrigue reimbursements. This will furnish you with the net benefit and will permit you to discover how a lot of cash you have made over the said period.

At long last, one ought to likewise set out on setting up the asset report as a significant aspect of the accounting framework. This framework will watch out for all the benefits and liabilities of one's business procedure. As such, just momentary obligations consider in the derivation of comprehensive resources. The long haul liabilities are placed in as though they were view as resources. Keeping precise bookkeeping records while directing business is essential for promoting and activity purposes, chiefly when one needs to submit statutory records and tax-related reports. It is useful for the company, and one should ensure that one fully informs regarding the record-keeping part and accounting documentation perspectives to forestall issues like tax avoidance and misrepresentation.

Online Bookkeepers Remote Accounting and Save Cost

Businesses everywhere throughout the world are attempting to work in an increasingly lean and proficient way. That implies a significant decrease in staff solidarity to diminish the overhead costs. Redistributing has been in vogue for quite a while for parts required for machines and mechanical items. In computerization, all finished and moment correspondence having become conceivable redistributing work spread to different divisions and online bookkeepers go under this class. Productive bookkeeping is the spine of the organization and auditing by a certified firm having become a statutory need; the estimation of valid booking is very evident. The online bookkeepers assume this crucial job.

Bookkeeping is a widely inclusive work covering all parts of maintaining a business. No division can work without cash, and each penny that comes in and goes out must be appropriately represented and recorded. One of the critical elements of bookkeepers, whether the organization or the online bookkeepers, is to update the administration as often as possible of store necessities on an everyday premise. They are additionally required to set up the reinforcement statements and necessary day to manage banks and other financial foundations for satisfactory and timely progression of assets. The online bookkeepers need to work quickly and effectively because all work finishes with an anonymous client.

The online bookkeepers are re-appropriating firms working for the customers legitimately on the web; they are sponsored by exceptionally qualified, experienced, and submitted people, both in bookkeeping and programming offices. This is the most fundamental prerequisites of every single online bookkeeper, particularly on the off chance that you are managing the client. The customer passes on the work toward the day's end and will expect the final result on his PC at the opening time the following day. The product utilized must be sufficient, work quickly, and set up all the announcements, discover abnormalities assuming any, and give solutions to many accounting issues.

The online bookkeepers work for various kinds and classes of clients. Some solitary arrangements with corporate though other people like to bargain smaller business houses, others have a blend of both. Bookkeepers have their purposes behind the decision of customers. However, every one of them is very clear around one part of their work, and that is work to complete fulfillment, whether huge or small. There is a lot of work for all because productive bookkeeping is the foundation for the successful running of any business adventure.

And motionless, at the end of the day, the mushrooming of many online bookkeepers in this manner makes disarray in the field. The issue isn't exceptionally hard to handle; however, it can be gotten over as nothing of outcome. It is to notice that all organizations in which adventure into the field are set up with capable qualified and experienced individuals. Consequently, it is an issue of how you present yourself to would-be clients with records of work done by you and being finished by you for your current clients. Best case scenario, you can consider it a solid challenge prompting you to show improvement over what you have been doing as such far.

Outsourcing Bookkeeping
and Administration

The choice of whether to redistribute - especially organization and bookkeeping, can be a difficult choice for some entrepreneurs.

Why?

From one perspective, it requires some investment, exertion, and different abilities to play out these obligations in any case appropriately; the allurement for the business person's to "handle it themselves" is frequently exceptionally influential.

Settling on a DECISION of how you will have your office organization and bookkeeping managed - is a significant inquiry to your corporate.

It is harmless to about that you are battling with the topic of redistributing your office organization and bookkeeping?

You have heard the total of the upsides and downsides, yet you, despite everything, need ILLEGAL STEPS to settle on a choice and push ahead?

Does your present circumstance discover you:

Planning your new business, however, not having the option to understand on the off chance that you have to have organization and bookkeeping set up.

Planning your new business, and you realize that you need office organization and bookkeeping done. However, you don't know some solution for it.

Have a business. However, you are always unable to get your business office organization and bookkeeping finished and done on schedule.

Progressively baffled with the time and bother it takes to play out your organization's office organization and bookkeeping in-house and know there is a superior way.

For what reason Do Entrepreneur's Need to Think About Office Administration and Bookkeeping?

In the first place, office organization is one of the most neglected parts of the new business visionary - yet it ought not to be!

Frequently the issue is the business visionary doesn't have the opportunity, capacity, or want to perform office organization, and they don't know what different alternatives that they have.

Now and then, business people don't understand what office organization includes and why it is fundamental to their business.

By and large, most businesses have:

An immense measure of information, documentation, and action that must be channeled through the business.

There should be regulatory procedures and frameworks set up all together for the business to work appropriately every day.

The business likewise should be overseen viably, and it depends on effective authoritative frameworks to help accomplish this.

For what reason is Bookkeeping So Important?

Sadly, numerous business people don't understand what a bookkeeping framework is for. Regularly, they think bookkeeping frameworks are an irrelevant piece of their business. They think they have an alternative not to have a bookkeeping framework - however, nothing could be further from reality.

All business proprietors commit to having a bookkeeping framework that exhibits the entirety of their business exchanges in a compact and valid organization.

A decent fundamental bookkeeping framework will at least:

- To record the sum attributable to the organization, that is debt claims
- To record the sum owed to outsiders, that is creditor liabilities
- To record the inflows and surges of money.

Thus, the choice is you will play out this in-house or re-appropriate to another individual or organization.

Recall that in-house alludes to the business playing out these obligations themselves. In any case, this could imply that the proprietor business person him/herself might be the individual playing out this, or they may procure low maintenance or full-time employee to work in their business, and they dole out this work to them. Redistributing is the hiring of an outside gathering to be paid to handle this.

Hence, the following stage is:

1. For each business visionary to welcome the requirement for good office organization framework and to decide whether this ought to be cultivated in-house or outsourced to an outsider and,

2. To perceive the requirement for a quality bookkeeping framework and to decide whether this ought to be cultivated in-house or outsourced.

The prior in your innovative life that you know this and settle on a DECISION - the better you will be over the long haul.

- With the goal for you to push ahead with this choice you have to:
- Truly value the requirement for appropriate organization and bookkeeping frameworks.
- Settle on a genuine DECISION concerning the redistributing of your organization and bookkeeping.
- Challenge your intuition as far as what you want to REALISTICALLY do in-house for your business.
- Truly survey your capacities regarding playing out your business organization and bookkeeping and why you may need to reexamine them.
- Acknowledge what engages with PROPER organization and bookkeeping frameworks.

Have activity steps to push you ahead and prevent you from "over-breaking down" the re-appropriating question.

How to Save Your Business Money by Outsourcing Your Bookkeeping and Administration Systems

Each business huge or little is presently concentrating on one primary concern: setting aside cash.

One of the significant suggestions made by profession bodies is to re-appropriate where conceivable. Outsourcing has a prompt diminishing impact on business overheads by supplanting costly salaried staff with the assistance that you can use as and when you need it.

One such assistance is accounting and office administration. In-house accounts offices are viewed as an extravagance for some, little or medium-sized organizations nowadays, and the ongoing upswing in organizations outsourcing things like payroll administration, invoicing, and accounting has been noted by many.

Rather than paying somebody full or even low maintenance to work in-house, it is unmistakably increasingly efficient to employ an organization to come in and manage your month-end, invoicing, or Payroll as required. Along these lines, there are no business commitments to stress over, and, when it hushes up, you don't need to pay representatives to lounge around sitting idle.

Re-appropriated administrations are typically adaptable, so they fit in with the requirements of any business. As a customer, you can single out what you need to do and when so the administrations fold over your particular needs, and you don't need to pay for the time that is not used.

Any business hoping to make impressive investment funds on their business running expenses would do well to re-appropriate things like VAT returns, CIS work, regularly scheduled Payroll, or in any event, composing letters, creating solicitations, and buy requests or anything accounts or administrator related.

Choosing Payroll Software and Accounting Solutions for Business

Online Bookkeepers - more and all the more independent companies are springing up. Not at all, like the multi-million dollar organizations, not every person can procure proficient payroll faculty. On paper, bookkeeping is gone to eradicate, and nowadays, independent ventures require bookkeeping payroll programming arrangements that assist them with setting aside time and cash at the same time.

Business bookkeeping programming plan program:

The business bookkeeping programming arrangements you get ought to incorporate the most recent payroll charge computations.

The product you buy should spare time for you and your organization.

The payroll bookkeeping programming you use ought to guarantee similarity checks, solicitations, proclamations, printable inventory, payroll tax documents, and that's only the tip of the iceberg.

Regardless of how much income your organization produces, you need a bookkeeping programming for your independent company with the chance that you have under 500 workers.

Ensure it has ongoing modules which you can customize and alter, contingent upon the number of administrators inside a similar document. This assists with staying up with the latest and effectively open.

The customer server budgetary bookkeeping frameworks you utilize should be compact to more than 600 various types of stages. Good with an IBM Z90® arrangement Mainframe to a 32 or 64 Bit Windows. This is the most significant factor in picking a business bookkeeping programming arrangement.

Ensure you can get the most recent five-year relative or the earlier week's deals, or the most recent two years inventories, at the snap of a catch.

Does the product ease everyday assignments? Ensure the product's enhancements, assuming any, are created on account of client and accomplice recommendations.

Accounting programming ought to have a climax of general record, checks and payroll bookkeeping, creditor liabilities, sometime later diary, and records receivable and payroll framework.

The product ought not to be unbending. It ought to have the option to oblige a wide range of custom reports. If yours is a little, however, developing an organization, the product's module joining must be phenomenal.

The review programming should be adaptable enough to have the option to deal with high volume information passage. Bookkeepers typically enter data either through a 'heads-up' or through a 'heads-down' mode. The product you purchase ought to have multi-state payroll preparing highlights.

Indeed, it's not about how costly or how may highlights it has, consistently searches for referrals, and read tributes to see if this is the product you need.

Most independent companies utilize less incredible frameworks. You can lead with keeping up all data online progressively by utilizing modules, for example,

- General Ledger
- Records Payable
- Records Receivable
- Bank Reconciliation
- Bound together Payroll
- Deterioration
- Stock Management
- Occupation Management
- Request Billing

Among all bookkeeping review programming, the least complex and generally effective to utilize are:

1. Customer Data Center

2. Payroll Service Bureau

3. Business

4. Temporary worker Management

The primary concern is, the customer server bookkeeping bundle ought to be easy to-utilize, have the option to report arranging, methodical, and focus on its ongoing perspective.

Advantages of QuickBooks Integration - For Businesses and Accounting Firms

80% of independent companies use QuickBooks to deal with their bookkeeping needs. This incorporates creditor liabilities, accounts receivables, time following, seller databases, and customer databases. QuickBooks is a progressive program that has one major blemish; it doesn't take into consideration local bringing in different frameworks of information.

Most business and their bookkeeping firms have no clue that they can bring anything into QuickBooks with a little assistance from a custom-programming firm. By coordinating divergent frameworks with QuickBooks, organizations can expand their profitability and run all the more proficiently by dispensing with excess information section.

Advantages to Small and Medium-Sized Businesses Utilizing QuickBooks

#1 Data is Entered Only Once

QuickBooks coordination implies that the information just must be entered once. When the information is gone into an organization's timekeeping or request section framework, there is no compelling reason to do much else. The information is likewise gone into QuickBooks continuously, which means fewer working hours and more proficiency.

#2 Fewer Errors

There are fewer information passage blunders when QuickBooks mix to use, as there is less human information section required. People commit errors, and the capacity to wipe out repetitive information sections will diminish these blunders.

#3 Enhanced Cash Flow

QuickBooks reconciliation takes into consideration quicker work processes from the purpose of section to the charging stage, which permits the business to charge quicker and increment income.

Advantages to Accounting Firms

#1 Emotional Capital

By encouraging QuickBooks coordination for its customers, bookkeeping firms will be seen as issue solvers by their customers. Being viewed as a guide that can help with expansive regions of the business, will prompt more referrals and progressively generally work for each firm.

#2 Fewer Errors

Since the data naturally refreshed, bookkeeping firms will find that there are fewer blunders in their customers' QuickBooks records. This abatement in blunders and time spent adjusting data will permit the bookkeeping firm to work quicker and all the more gainfully.

#3 Files Will Be Received Earlier

Bookkeeping firms will find that their customers will hand over their QuickBooks records prior, which will permit the organizations to deal with the bustling assessment seasons effortlessly.

#4 Higher Rate Accounting Work

Since customers will spend less cash on accounting administrations, bookkeeping firms who prescribe QuickBooks coordination will see that these equivalent customers presently have bigger spending plans for higher rate bookkeeping work.

Techniques

There are two fundamental strategies used to encourage QuickBooks joining. These are group imports and backend reconciliation. With group imports, the entrepreneur can make a fare document, see the substance, and afterward decide to bring that record into QuickBooks. With backend incorporation, the two frameworks converse with one another legitimately, implying that all are finished progressively.

Genuine instances of organizations that can profit by QuickBooks combination are bookkeeping firms, staffing offices that use time following frameworks to pay their representatives, online stores who sell items on the web and afterward should record the business information for the bookkeeping, and enormous development organizations that use complex work request frameworks.

A trustworthy custom programming firm can use to incorporate QuickBooks into most web applications or work area applications. This coordination empowers little and medium-sized organizations to develop by lessening worker hours, expanding proficiency, and improving organization profitability.

Onsite Bookkeeping and Offsite Bookkeeping Services Explained

Generally, small to medium organizations needn't bother with a full-time accountant. Most low maintenance clerks that these organizations contract by and large don't stay for long. These organizations complete their work by a bookkeeping firm.

For the most part, a bookkeeping firm gives two sorts of administrations, Onsite bookkeeping administrations and Offsite bookkeeping administrations. This article will clarify in detail what every one of these administrations is, and what their advantages and disadvantages resemble.

For onsite bookkeeping, an accountant genuinely goes to work in the business place. It is, to some degree, like the clerk that you employ with certain distinctions. The bookkeeping firm sends an accountant to the customer's office.

Onsite bookkeeping administration has a few preferences. The greatest preferred position is the cash you spare by enlisting somebody just for the days you need.

At the point when you have this sort of administration, you don't need to stay with a similar accountant if you think he/she isn't functioning admirably for you. Call the secure and you can have an alternate individual working for you. At the point when you locate the ideal clerk, you can request that the firm send a similar individual to work. You never find a workable pace if you procure a clerk.

Another benefit is that you don't feel essential to stress over representative advantages. You pay straightforwardly to the bookkeeping firm, so there is no check included.

Bookkeeping and Taxation rules are mind boggling, and risks are most accountants don't have the foggiest idea about these guidelines. At the point when you get an onsite administration, there are different clerks that your accountant can pose inquiries to. A large portion of these organizations is prepared on their toes to support them.

There are a few drawbacks to onsite bookkeeping as well. Onsite bookkeeping administration contrasts, starting with one bookkeeping firm then onto the next. A few firms have base assistance buy necessity. For instance, this may imply that you should get in any event a specific number of days of the week to have the option to get onsite administration.

Since your onsite accountant isn't occupied all day for you, you will, in any case, need to do some work like assembly solicitations and bills when the person isn't working.

For Offsite bookkeeping, the bookkeeping firm takes every necessary step in their office. This sort of administration is additionally called virtual bookkeeping administration (no, it's anything but a PC working for you, a genuine individual takes a shot at your documents). Essentially, it seems as though your accountant's office is away from your business area. You should send your records like solicitations, charges, bank explanations, and so forth to the bookkeeping firm.

The principle bit of leeway of offsite bookkeeping is the expense of administration. It is shockingly less expensive (as modest as $50 every month) than onsite bookkeeping administration. If you can't bear to get a clerk, you ought to, in any event, get offsite bookkeeping administration. With these costs, it is practically strange not to do bookkeeping or attempt to do the bookkeeping yourself.

A few firms send their express dispatch administration to get your archives. On the off chance that you are PC adroit, you can examine your reports and email or transfer them to their site. You can likewise fax your archives. While sending an enormous number of solicitations, bills, and articulations by email or fax look additional tedious, these techniques are acceptable when you need to send a couple of archives, similar to a missing receipt, or the bank explanation, and so forth.

Continuously affirm what administrations are incorporated when purchasing offsite bookkeeping administrations. Some firm doesn't give payroll administration or assessment settlement administration when you purchase the ordinary offsite bookkeeping administration. Some furnish you with month to month reports while different firms may very well give your yearly reports.

Another significant thing to recall is to ensure you comprehend what programming your bookkeeping firm employments. Even though we as a whole like clerks with quite a while or even many years of experience, they may be utilizing programming that is obsolete or practically obsolete. At the hour of composing this article, QuickBooks and Simply Accounting are the two most well-known programming that most accountants are utilizing.

At long last, Stay away from locally established business accountants except if you are certain beyond a shadow of a doubt about the nature of their administration. They may stop their administration whenever later on, and you may be left with your unusable business information.

Hiring a Bookkeeper: 8 Accounting Interview Questions To Ask

Hiring an accountant can be a staggering procedure for some small entrepreneurs. Before you start the pursuit, it's essential to decide the sort of experience and abilities you need. It is benign to say that you are searching for somebody to examine the numbers for you and make a spending limit or do you extremely simply need somebody to information to enter the bills and solicitations?

With the chance that you have somebody to assist you with understanding the numbers, or you have a solid bookkeeping and money related administration foundation, getting an individual who is capable of your bookkeeping programming and whose experience and character is a fit for your business will likely turn out well. Then again, if you don't have anybody ensuring the numbers are right, the information passage clerk is anything but a smart thought. Right now, I need to search for somebody with full charge bookkeeping experience. That is, the capacity accommodates the adjust and play out a month to month close. Ordinarily, clerks don't have the range of abilities to assist you with monetary administration past exact money related reports.

When you place a promotion, you'll be blessed to receive a buffet of candidates. You'll need to limit the heap of candidates to the individuals who address the issues of your set of working responsibilities, and then the interviewing fun will start. You'll need to ask questions that will guarantee the accountant truly has the correct aptitudes and will fit the way of life of your business. Here are eight questions to ask your potential clerk:

1) Do you think gathering or money premise detailing is better for business the executives?

Search for a propelled clerk to clarify that gathering premise bookkeeping gives better monetary reports. However, money premise is normally favored for charges. We can keep the books on accumulation reason for the executives detailing and the duty bookkeeper can make modifications for money premise charges. A standard accountant will presumably mention to you what her experience has been and won't have an inclination for either.

2) What is the bookkeeping condition (or the accounting report condition) or clarify the monetary record?

A decent clerk will clarify the monetary record has resources, liabilities, and value. This is mandatory for anybody you hope to give exact money related reports. In a perfect world, they will disclose to you the condition is Assets = Liabilities + Equity. On the off chance that they can't clarify the monetary record, at that point, ask them to portray an advantage and obligation account. You won't need somebody who doesn't have the foggiest idea about the accounting report liable for month-end close, however on the off chance that another person is guaranteeing exactness, simply knowing how resources and liabilities used will be fine.

3) The financial balance is off $0.72. To what extent will you spend searching for the issue, and what steps will you take to discover it?

This issue is dubious and truly relies upon what you might want to find in the correct clerk. Some won't stop looking until they discover it. Without a doubt, there could be various things causing any inconsistency so you do need them to invest some energy searching for the issue. Yet, what amount of time? Is going through 2 hours searching for $.72 the best utilization of time? If we take a gander at the rate of return, that is a terrible utilization of time. On the off chance that they answer 2 hours, you'll need to research their tolerance for non-immaculate conditions. In case you're in the inventive field, an extraordinary stickler may make you crazy. Assuming, in any case, they won't search for the blunder by any stretch of the imagination, their scrupulousness presumably isn't sufficient, and you should continue looking.

When searching for the error, the perfect candidate will say it's probably a transposition blunder, and they would begin there first (transposition mistakes are distinguishable by 9). They may say they would check each detail against the announcement, which is consummately substantial.

4) in real money premise bookkeeping, how might your record a $600 yearly protection premium?

The correct response for money premise is charge protection cost $600, credit money, or records payable. All accountants ought to get this right.

5) How might you record a $600 yearly protection premium utilizing gathering bookkeeping?

The right response here is Debit Prepaid Insurance $600, Credit Cash or Accounts Payable. Nudge them to discover when protection cost is perceived. It ought to be $50/month with a Debit to Insurance Expense and a Credit to Prepaid Insurance. On the off chance that the candidate can't address this inquiry, don't anticipate that they should keep your books dependent on an accumulation bookkeeping. You will need to rely upon another person for the executive's reports.

6) what number corner stores (or coffeehouses, and so forth) do you think there are in the U.S.?

With this inquiry, we're searching for acceptable basic reasoning abilities. It's not alright to figure a number with no clarification or to state they would "google" it. You need the candidate to have a procedure for finding a good pace, regardless of how far away it is. There are numerous corner stores in my town, and I would figure out these numerous towns in my state.

7) Rank the accompanying arranged by significance for business achievement: Sales, Teamwork, Quality, Integrity, Profitability, Service

There is not a set in stone response to this inquiry. However, it will show whether the candidate is lined up with your business culture and additionally exhibit basic reasoning aptitudes. Search for support for why they addressed how they fixed. Does it line up with how you would respond to the inquiry? For instance, if they state Profitability is the most significant. Why would that be the situation? On the off chance that they state collaboration is least significant, you likely need to burrow somewhat more profound if cooperation is high on your need list.

A clerk would ideally list gainfulness lower on the rundown since you need to realize that they are thinking about the entire business, not simply their activity. You would likewise need to see trustworthiness high on the rundown. Do you truly need a clerk who doesn't esteem respectability?

8) Tell me about a period you didn't concur with something your supervisor asked you to do.

The correct answer here will rely on the character you're chasing. Do you need a devotee who will do what you state? Is it true that you are searching for a counselor to mention to you what ought to finish? Maybe a blend is a correct response for you, somebody who is sufficiently sure to express their genuine thoughts, yet is eager to take the course.

Quickbooks Help and Accounts Receivable Issue

On the off chance that you are responsible for keeping the monetary records of a business, a decent bookkeeping program is an absolute necessity. Numerous lawful and budgetary prerequisites exist in today's business world and utilizing programming as Quickbooks permits you to remain sorted out and give you convenient reports. Having your business in a great budgetary request is an absolute necessity particularly as duty time draws near. At the point when you need help with the application you are utilizing to be certain you are precisely recording and announcing information getting Quickbooks to assist will with being a decent move to make.

The records receivable zone of Quickbooks is where missteps can be disturbing as well as exorbitant. A mix-up right now causes cash owed to you to stay unpaid or in any event, paying too much in charges and nobody needs that botch. As duty opportunity arrives around, getting Quickbooks help is the ideal approach to be sure that you don't overpay the legislature because of basic bookkeeping botches that could have effectively maintained a strategic distance.

Does your records receivable look off base? At the opinion when you take a gander at your records receivable adjust and can tell that it isn't right yet can't explain why this is no uncertainty a blunder in your Quickbooks documents. At the point when your rundown of customers and what they owe shown and yet the parity is off base, this normally prompts long stretches of disappointment and investigating and over the information attempting to make sense of where you turned out badly. On the off chance that you have gazed at your Quickbooks sufficiently long and can't discover the needle in the sheaf, it's likely time to bring in some help.

A typical mistake happens when you realize that a customer account comes up with all required funds, and yet they show an equalization. This can distort their benefit or misfortune sum. To show precise fiscal summaries, the equalization in your Quickbooks records of sales must be right. If a customer shows a negative equalization in their Accounts Receivable, that customer has overpaid their record and has a credit balance. If this is erroneous, at that point, the equalization in the record is inaccurate. At the point when a receipt isn't made and recorded; however, an installment is recorded, the equalization will show inaccurate. You could have sent the receipt and got installment, yet on the off chance that you disregard to record the receipt in your Quickbooks, the records receivable total will not be right. Receipt mistakes can likewise happen if an installment is applied against an inappropriate receipt or under an inappropriate customer.

Indeed, even a mix-up as basic as one letter can cause a glitch in your whole bookkeeping framework if blunders are made. If you have a customer called "Bill's Boat Repair," you should make certain to spell the business name the equivalent each time you include a record for the customer. That you coincidentally call the business "Bill's Boat Repairs" in your Quickbooks records, it will be perceived as a different record. Simply including or erasing an "s" toward the finish of a name can cause a disparity in your documents.

You are an accountant that needs to keep great budgetary records productively for your business utilizing Quickbooks is the best approach. Utilizing the product can be tested alone. The ideal approach to abstain from overpaying charges or long periods of dissatisfaction is by utilizing Texas Quickbooks Help to go over your Quickbooks records and guarantee your business' money related achievement.

Business Bookkeeping Guidelines and Acquiring Bookkeeping Support

If you resemble many small entrepreneurs, you begin out by playing out your one of a kind bookkeeping and may well even set up your association assessment form. This possibly an overwhelming action is constraining you to hold up until the last moment before charge time to get your budgetary records together. Probably the greatest reason for organization disappointment is poor record keeping. With Promoting and selling, customer relations, organizing and above all, overseeing items or administrations, you straightforward may maybe not have the opportunity to concentrate on your bookkeeping and bookkeeping records. You require well-kept records for charge readiness, overseeing the development and to show how appropriately the business is getting along. As you arrangement your bookkeeping program, you may likewise need to found systems for monitoring your records.

With your small business is new, it might be particularly hard for an arrangement and hold your books. It's anything but an awesome thought for another association to utilize checkbooks and receipts as their bookkeeping framework. There are numerous clerks and bookkeepers around which will offer bookkeeping backing should you tend not to have the opportunity to finish your books. Recorded here are some significant bookkeeping suggestions which will help small entrepreneurs:

Become Acquainted with your bookkeeping program.

Regardless of whether you procure an inward or outer clerk, it tends to be significant that you have an understanding of the numbers created out of your program. One of the most notable bookkeeping programming bundles accessible available as of now is QuickBooks. On the off chance that you use QuickBooks bookkeeping programming, a clerk or bookkeeper can give essential instruction on your product program that can be very definitely justified even despite the cash and time contributed. You have to understand the essential components of your bookkeeping project, for example, general record, an outline of records, payroll, invoicing creditor liability and records receivable.

Build up Bookkeeping Procedures and Internal Controls

Untrustworthy faculty can slow down your business or put you bankrupt. It truly is fundamental to have effective inside controls in position and foundation, a decent method of approaches and systems to oversee interior controls. Interior control strategies should likewise evaluate routinely to safeguard that it truly is cutting-edge. Broadly educate others inside the organization to handle bookkeeping once the representative handling the books take some time off or wiped out leave. This can be common when misappropriation is found. Hiring an outside bookkeeping firm to evaluate your books all the time can commonly be an incredible interior to keep away from worker burglary.

Outsourcing your Bookkeeping

For any individual who is curious about setting up and keeping up your books and must have bookkeeping help going ahead, outsourcing may be a decision. Bookkeeping, payroll and expense arrangement can redistribute to free accountants or bookkeeping organizations having some expertise in these areas. It may be a decent idea to oversee day by day or week after week deals, inventory and inside revealing; however, you may utilize a certified clerk or bookkeeper to see your books all the time. That you choose to redistribute these capacities, guarantee that your records are promptly available to you.

Make Timely and Useful budget reports

At the point when your bookkeeping programming is arrangement viable, you have an astounding bookkeeping framework set up. At the point when you and your inward clerk prepare on bookkeeping programming, for example, QuickBooks, it can produce opportune and handy fiscal reports. You ought to produce fiscal reports on a month to month, quarterly and yearly premise. Budget summaries comprise of a benefit and misfortune proclamation, accounting report and income explanation.

Another organization proprietor can get a bookkeeping programming bundle and have it customized for their business. Most small entrepreneurs may conceivably not have the opportunity to play out this themselves and require outside help from somebody who has practical experience in their preferred bookkeeping programming bundle.

Bookkeeping Services from External Professionals are Highly Reliable and Affordable

Bookkeeping and bookkeeping are among the real all-inclusive factors of business the executives. Various business visionaries without fundamental preparation in any zone of business the executives feel no association at all with number juggling and figures. The vast majority of them exceed expectations effectively in systems administration and showcasing yet not continuing bookkeeping books. This is when bookkeeping administrations start to sound good to them. The conventional method for getting your books kept is hiring an inward accountant. The in-house worker is the present view as an overwhelming weight that generally forthcoming and recently shaped organizations can't withstand.

Consistently they need compensation. You have both settled upon whether your business makes enough benefits or not. There comes when in-house representatives need to leave on a paid leave too. Preparing and pre-preparing is additionally their lawful right, not to overlook that representatives are likewise qualified for laborers' remuneration and different advantages. You likewise need sufficient opportunity to direct execution evaluations to conclude who is qualified for advantages and rewards. To put it plainly, an inner accountant is a major lawful obligation that most new organizations need to avoid. Bookkeeping administrations from an outcast are significantly more solid.

At the point when the time to pick outer Bookkeeping administrations comes, you should conclude whom to employ between a consultant and bookkeeping firm. Specialists have not enrolled home organizations. They could be people who most likely sidestep paying charges themselves. Then again, a bookkeeping organization is a properly enlisted business furnished with many ensured clerks, office gear, most recent accountant's product, and satisfactory office space in addition to other things. It constantly fits to pick Bookkeeping administrations that are offered by an authentic organization. Numerous errors could result due to do-it-without anyone else's help bookkeeping. So you are not encouraged to keep your books by and by on the off chance that you are not a prepared clerk or bookkeeper.

Fortunately, with the assistance of free Bookkeeping administration suppliers, you can abstain from committing expensive DIY bookkeeping errors. An outer clerk that you need to frame an agreement with ought to have an appropriate understanding of the bookkeeping and bookkeeping programming. These days of all shapes and sizes organizations are utilizing programming to spare time and produce exact work.

Moreover, your preferred supplier of Bookkeeping administrations must demonstrate their understanding of the fundamental bookkeeping standards and standards followed in your nation. This will assist you with maintaining a strategic distance from an issue with the law for submitting inappropriately done government forms or for coming up short on charges. They will likewise keep you refreshed with changes in expense guidelines in your industry.

For the most part, a re-appropriated clerk works from a remote office. So they anticipate that you should have the option to follow everyday exchanges and produce source archives like receipts. Many re-appropriated organizations offer online administrations. Their customers send checked source reports to them. So you should watch out for each exchange that your business may get every day to deliver the necessary source reports. Since they have huge groups of laborers, re-appropriated accountants balance your books quickly with the product you have picked. Bookkeeping Services suppliers are truly adept at pursuing solicitations. They will ensure that the solicitations you have sent customers respect on schedule and that the solicitations sent to you by providers clear on schedule.

Exact Bookkeeping Services improves the capacity of a firm to concentrate on business development while at the same time reducing dangers and expenses. There are numerous organizations offering bookkeeping administrations that work for small and medium organizations around the world.